WORLD PRAISE 2

Edited by David Peacock

LifeWay Press
Nashville, Tennessee

ISBN 0-6330-0701-3

Music and text set by Barnes Music Engraving Ltd.,
East Sussex, England, United Kingdom

Printed in the United States of America

FOREWORD

"O sing to the Lord a new song; sing to the Lord, all the earth!" (Psalm 96:1)

World Praise 2 is a collection of new songs from around the Christian world. The Psalmist commanded us to sing continuously praises to the Lord. The Christian is one who extols the love of God expressed in Jesus Christ through music and song. This collection includes new songs from Africa and Asia, Caribbean and Latin America, North America and Europe.

As we enter the 21st century one of the great facts of our time is that the numerical predominance of the Christian world is moving from Europe and North America to the two thirds world. Very often in these countries, new songs and music have arisen from the people and express in a wonderful way the joy of following Jesus Christ. In 1910 about 85% of Christians were from Europe and North America. In the year 2000 almost 60% of Christians are from the former mission fields of Africa, Asia, and Latin America! We need to listen to our brothers and sisters from so many different races, cultures and languages. We need to hear their cry of pain and their laughter of joy, their deep and personal way of thanking the Lord and expressing gratefulness for their salvation. We need to hear their cry for justice and their way of expressing these concerns in a Biblical and yet in a new way!

World Praise 2 is a special edition of songs from around the world, published specifically for the 18th Baptist World Congress held in Melbourne, Australia, January 5 9, 2000. However, because of previous experience with the popularity of our special edition of *World Praise* for the 1995 Baptist World Alliance Congress held in Buenos Aires, Argentina, we are pleased to make this edition available to the larger Christian public.

Words fail to express our appreciation to David Peacock of Great Britain for his outstanding work in editing this collection. The BWA has been grateful for his wonderful assistance in coordinating the music and worship of our last two congresses. His humble spirit, keen love for Christ and sensitivity to contextual concerns of Christians of many cultures combine to make his ministry of music an international exercise of educating all of us to a richer and broader experience of Christian music worldwide.

It is our prayer that this edition of *World Praise 2* will be found in the hands of many singing congregations worldwide. Certainly, we hope that their worship and praise to the triune God—Father, Son and Holy Spirit—will be enhanced as they sing their way through this book. Indeed, let us join with the Psalmist and all of humanity and sing a new song unto the Lord!

Denton Lotz
General Secretary
Baptist World Alliance

PREFACE

World Praise 2 is a unique collection of material drawn from worshiping communities around the world. Here you will find material from every continent—music that crosses denominations and traditions. The items have been chosen because of their ability to travel beyond their place of origin. They range from lively expressions of praise to quiet songs of confession to poignant items yearning for justice.

Texts for most items are in both the original language and in English. In the English translation we have attempted to convey the original meaning as far as possible while trying to fit the text into a regular metrical pattern. We would encourage congregations to sing in the original language wherever appropriate.

This newest volume of *World Praise* draws on material from the previous two editions and includes a number of additional items. The music is arranged with straightforward accompaniments that attempt to capture the authentic nature of each song. Vocal parts, where appropriate, are arranged in four parts. Guitar chords are given for most songs. Each item has performance notes so that congregations are able to sing the different styles of music with integrity. I am greatly indebted to Geoff Weaver, joint editor of the previous volume of *World Praise.* This edition draws heavily on his expertise, enthusiasm and involvement with indigenous worship music.

World Praise 2 can easily be used as a supplement to a congregation's existing repertoire. The book ideally is suited to churches seeking a global perspective within their worship and a broad repertoire for their worship expression. Many items work well alongside hymns and worship songs. *World Praise 2* is also useful for missionary services, for international conferences and cross-cultural events, and for congregations made up of a range of nationalities and cultures. The stimulus for this book comes from the Baptist World Alliance's Worship Commission, which is involved in researching different perspectives on worship around the world. As this edition was used for the first time at the 18th Baptist World Congress in Melbourne, a selection of recent Australian worship songs is included in a second section of the book.

In recent years, Christians in the West have begun to see mission as more of a partnership—a giving and receiving between different parts of the Body of Christ. Those of us who have so many resources of our own have found it difficult to imagine that we might need to receive from others—or indeed that there might be hidden riches for us to receive. *World Praise 2* is an opportunity to enrich our worship. In prayer, we can often react intellectually to news of suffering abroad. However, when we sing the songs of Christians in other parts of the world, we are able to enter more fully into their joys and pains. Then we truly understand what Paul means when he writes 'rejoice with those who rejoice and mourn with those who mourn' (Romans 12:15).

David Peacock

INTRODUCTION

The hymns, psalms, and spiritual songs contained in this edition of *World Praise 2* are more than just hymns, psalms, and spiritual songs. They are small windows into the spiritual lives and living cultures of Christians around the world. Looking and singing through these musical windows is an exciting experience in the discovery of how God has blessed and encouraged the people of his vast kingdom. The following pages are designed to help make singing as authentic as possible, especially for those rooted in a Western culture.

There are four basic areas which you should consider as you use this book. First, understand the cultural considerations of the different music. Second, prepare the church leadership, musicians, and congregation for the introduction of new music. Third, enjoy the music through thorough musical preparation. And fourth, introduce the music to your congregation in meaningful ways that will enhance each individual's worship experience and understanding of God's diverse kingdom.

Cultural Considerations

Linguistic scholars have long recognized the inseparability of language and culture. The same can be said for music and culture. The text of a song and the musical language used to carry the text are closely tied to how people live within their societal context. Cultures have "ways" of singing that influence directly how the music is used within a worship context.

For example, African songs are often circular with call and response singing. At the heart of African culture is the participatory nature of community. The music is highly functional, in that the perfect performance of the music is not as important as helping the congregation to express its praise, and to include all members in one voice. As such, improvisation and extraneous sounds allow participants to make their own unique contribution while remaining a part of the group. In the African context, singing a single song can last more than thirty minutes, while the music builds to high emotional expression. Although some cultures rely heavily on abstract hymn texts, many African cultures internalize the main theme, while the leader adds comments with his or her voice. The singer applies the simple and profound theme to his or her own life. When singing African selections, prepare the congregation for a joyous and relaxed participation without attention to perfection, so often the concern of classically trained musicians. Drums, rattles, shakers, bells, and clapping are effective instruments to accompany the singing. Two practices often inhibit the cultural experience of non-Western songs. The first is singing in English; the second, using the fixed pitch of the piano or organ. It is important in African songs specifically, and world songs in general, to try the song in its original language and without the confinement of a keyboard.

Asia is filled with many diverse cultures. Some of these cultures, as in parts of India and rural communities, sing songs more like the "round" music of Africa. However, India, China, and other parts of the Asian world have their own highly developed and written musical systems. These systems are closely tied to the historical religious systems of Hinduism, and the teachings of Confucius, Buddhism, and Islamic influences on art and music. The tonal languages found in many Asian culture groups also affect the scales, which have quartertones not found in Western systems. Therefore, they often sound "out-of-tune" to Western ears. The history and influence of these religious traditions has helped form a deep respect for the beauty of nature and the inner reflective quality of prayer and meditation. Like the beauty of a flower, music from these traditions is often more subtle with asymmetric phrases, vocal ornamentation, and unique timbres. As with African music, the keyboard is not the ideal instrument for accompaniment of most Asian hymns. Flutes, guitars, drums, gongs, and bells provide effective quality to the singing and help engender a more reflective atmosphere for focusing on the nature and meaning of the texts.

Similarly, Latin America is diverse, with many cultures. It is unique, however, in its strong "mestizo" nature of mixed cultures from Africa, Europe, and indigenous peoples. As a result, many songs from Latin America have highly rhythmic characteristics with buoyant, passionate melodies. If African music is more circular and participatory, and Asian music is often reflective, Latin hymns are often very festive and celebrate the day of the Lord with rejoicing, dancing, clapping, and many instruments. The resulting sound is celebrative, emotional, sensual, festive, and moving. Texts are filled with strong proclamation of the gospel in personal and community liberation. All forms of instruments are used to augment and to accompany the full-bodied singing. Guitars, congas, maracas, keyboards, flutes, and brass instruments drive this "fiesta" of God in worship.

While there is not space here to give specific "performance" practices of hundreds of world churches, this general description should emphasize the diversity of music making, and the necessity for understanding more than the notes of a musical page. Doing some research with a growing body of knowledge about this music is the first step in effective worship incorporation of *World Praise 2*.

Congregational Preparation

If music is cultural, it is also a major element of identity. We express our ethnic and denominational loyalty by the music we sing. We also have individual preferences which are quite strong. Many people hold dearly to the music which they first experience when they become followers of the Christian faith. So, to most people, learning new music to the exclusion of their own is an unwelcome change.

At a recent international music workshop 100 musicians, pastors, and lay leaders from many different ethnic communities were asked what they experienced as the greatest barriers to incorporating international songs into their worship. Their first responses were not surprising. They cited generational preferences, resistance to change, a lack of motivation and knowledge, poorly equipped musicians, and intimidation by new and sometimes different sounds as the major barriers.

Considering the resistance to change, the task of the worship leader is to effectively prepare the congregation for new music, of any kind. Introduction of new music can be a fun and exciting addition to the worship experience. The following guidelines will aid in preparing the congregation and introducing the hymns of *World Praise 2.*

Change begins first with the realization and awareness that God's kingdom is vast and diverse. As part of the broader global church, we have a responsibility to relate to our brothers and sisters of many cultures in hymns of our past, hymns of the present, and hymns from those who call themselves followers of Christ, yet come from different cultures and ethnic groups.

Second, most congregations will try anything new if they have a trusting relationship with their musicians and worship leaders. This trust begins with the experience that worship leaders are interested in the musical well-being and personal ministry of the person in the pew. This trust is built on the use of music not sung for the sake of change or novelty, but for the sincere enhancement of the worship experience. Trust is built slowly, through the effective introduction of new songs which supplement current experience, as opposed to supplanting it. Trust is also built when congregations are prepared for new music. This preparation comes from involving the congregation in the process through worship planning committees, congregational rehearsals, and positive musical experiences. Repeat the music often, until it becomes comfortable and a part of the church's musical repertoire.

Musical Preparation

One way in which congregations best receive new hymns and songs is through well-rehearsed and well-presented music. The use of a choir, soloist, or music group that has prepared the music well in advance will go a long way toward helping the congregation feel comfortable in singing a new song. The following guidelines will aid the preparation of individual music items prior to the introduction to the church congregation.

The text is the primary focus of the song. Understanding the meaning brings an equal acceptance of the music. When singing a hymn or song in the original language, be sure to provide a translation for the singers and congregation. If possible, sing the song in both its original language and the language of the congregation. Learn the correct pronunciation and, if possible, provide a pronunciation guide to the congregation. Rehearse the pronunciation, slowly, before singing the item. Keep accompaniment under the voice so that the text is prominent and singers are not distracted.

Most people will alter a new melody to fit their existing style. If possible, keep the melody intact, especially if it has vocal ornamentation. You can aid in this learning by having an instrument play through the melody line. Many world hymns and songs are sung in unison or may have harmony unusual to the local ear. Teaching the choir, or small group, first will aid in the congregation's efforts to sing in a new musical language.

As indicated in the cultural descriptions above, instruments enhance the presentation of songs. They also incorporate members of the congregation into the singing. Where possible, use appropriate instruments and minimize dependence on the piano and organ.

Many trained musicians are concerned with the correct "style" and performance of a hymn or song. However, in many non-Western traditions it is not the correct "performance" of the item that is important, but the spiritual experience of the hymn or song. Therefore, consider playing a recording or video of the hymn to help in the learning. Because movement is vital to many hymns, especially those of Africa and Latin America, help the shy and reflective congregation to join in. Teach the choir the movement and clapping patterns. Then, invite the congregation to participate.

Finally, in introducing the song to the congregation, some may want to consider an introduction of national and local culture, and information about the local Christian community. If possible, with a little research, find the story of the hymn. Since many hymns are the personal testimonies of Christians, the story will enhance the congregation's appreciation. Although be careful to avoid this becoming just an educative exercise, rather than a natural part of a worship flow.

Enhanced Worship Experience

World Praise 2 hymns and songs provide a basis for the total worship experience as preludes, offertories, and special music selections, as well as congregational songs. With creative worship planning, these hymns and songs can serve to enhance exciting processionals, thoughtful and meditative prayer responses, exciting choir specials, and vibrant congregational singing. Utilizing these items is also an excellent tool to reach out into your local community. Within the immediate context of most churches are musicians from different ethnic groups who can be invited to assist in the preparation and presentation of the music. In the process, the local congregation has a way to interact with the people of the music. With the advantage of the Internet, contacts can even be made with musicians in the country of origin.

The primary purpose of *World Praise 2* is not to provide a tourist view of world hymnody. It is an honest and sincere effort to enhance the worship experience of the local church. As such, consider using these hymns and songs in ways that draw the congregation into fellowship with God and fellow believers around the world. When church congregations around the world can sing with Christians of other cultural traditions, they truly begin to worship God in world praise.

J. Nathan Corbitt is the author of *The Sound of the Harvest, Music's Mission in Church and Culture* (Baker Books, 1998).

LEGAL INFORMATION AND ACKNOWLEDGEMENTS

We are grateful to all those who have provided material for this volume. We especially thank those belonging to Baptist churches around the world and to mission partners of the Church Missionary Society, from whom many of the songs have been collected. We particularly wish to acknowledge the late Michael Perry for his expertise in adapting many texts, and our thanks to Laura Werts for preparing the material for publication. For the major task of copyright clearance we are deeply grateful to Toby Baxley. We are also grateful to John Fearn-Wannan for his assistance in the collection of material from Australia, and to Mike Mack-Smith and Barnes Music Engraving. Special thanks to Dr. Terry C. Terry, Sharron Lyon and the staff at LifeWay Christian Resources for their work in coordinating the publication of this book.

Every effort has been made to trace copyright owners, and apologies are extended to anyone whose rights have inadvertently not been acknowledged. Any omissions or inaccuracies of copyright details will be corrected in future editions.

Reprinting
Those seeking to reprint material in this book should refer to the addresses given at the back of the book.

SECTION 1:

HYMNS AND SONGS

OF THE

WORLDWIDE CHURCH

1 ALL WHO ARE THIRSTY

PHILIPPINES

Words: from Isaiah 55
Michael Perry
Music: Mutya Lopez Solis
arranged Geoff Weaver

Steadily ♩ = 92
Dm
A
1 All who are thirs - ty,___ come to the Lord,
2 Why spend your mon - ey,___ yet have no bread;
3 Call on God's mer - cy___ while he is near,
4 Where once were bri - ers,___ flo-wers will grow,
A7
Dm
all who are hun - gry,___ feed on his word;
why work for noth - ing?___ Trust God in-stead!
turn from your e - vil,___ come with-out fear;
where lives were bar - ren,___ riv - ers will flow:
D
Gm
buy with-out pay - ing,___ food with-out price,
He will pro-vide you___ rich-est of food:
ask him for par - don –___ grace will a-bound!
praise to our Sav - ior:___ grace and re-nown –

Typically Filipino in its blend of joy and melancholy, this song speaks of the hope that Filipino Christians, so often hit by suffering and oppression, have in Christ. A guitar accompaniment is very effective here.

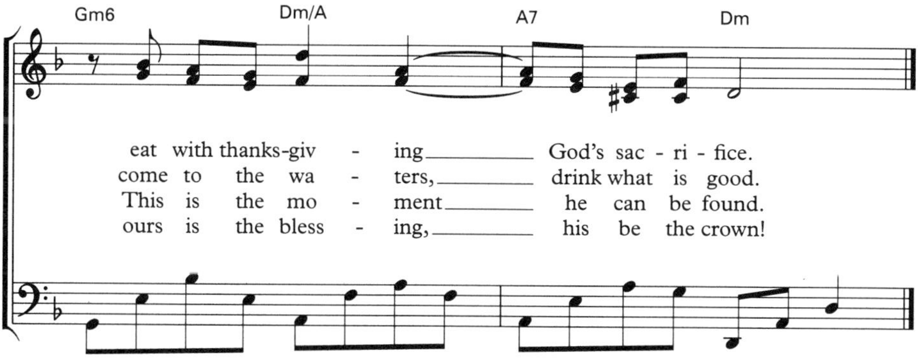
Gm6 Dm/A A7 Dm
eat with thanks-giv - ing God's sac - ri - fice.
come to the wa - ters, drink what is good.
This is the mo - ment he can be found.
ours is the bless - ing, his be the crown!

1 All who are thirsty, come to the Lord,
all who are hungry, feed on his word;
buy without paying, food without price,
eat with thanksgiving God's sacrifice.

2 Why spend your money, yet have no bread;
why work for nothing? Trust God instead!
He will provide you richest of food:
come to the waters, drink what is good.

3 Call on God's mercy while he is near,
turn from your evil, come without fear;
ask him for pardon – grace will abound!
This is the moment he can be found.

4 Where once were briers, flowers will grow,
where lives were barren, rivers will flow:
praise to our Savior: grace and renown –
ours is the blessing, his be the crown!

2 ALLELUIA

SOUTH AFRICA

Words: traditional liturgical text
Music: unknown
transcribed from the singing of George Mxadana

Warmly and purposefully ♩ = 96

Al - le - lu - ia, al - le - lu - ia.
Al - le - lu - ia, al - le - lu - ia. Al -
-le - lu - ia, al - le - lu - ia. Al -
-le - lu - ia, al - le - lu - ia.

South Africans are renowned for the richness of their unaccompanied singing.
This should be sung reflectively rather than boisterously, and should be unaccompanied.

3 AMAHORO BENEDATA

Peace be with you

RWANDA

Words: unknown
Music: unknown
arranged Geoff Weaver

Medium tempo ♩ = 104

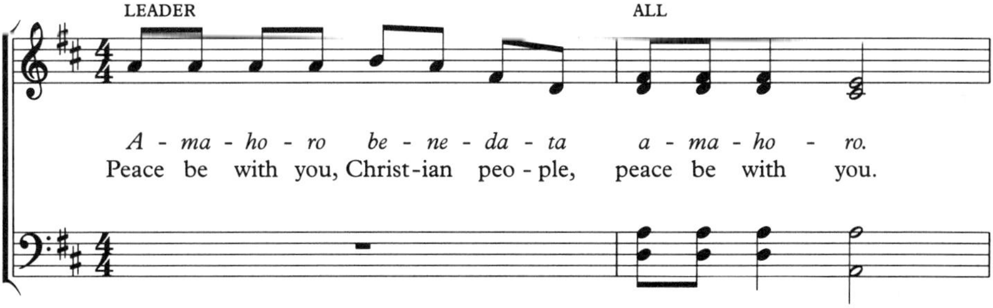
LEADER
ALL
A - ma - ho - ro be - ne - da - ta a - ma - ho - ro.
Peace be with you, Christ-ian peo - ple, peace be with you.

A - ma - ho - ro kwa Ye - su, a - ma - ho - ro – hal - le - lu - jah!
Peace be with you through Je - sus, peace be with you – hal - le - lu - jah!

1	LEADER	*Amahoro benedata*	1	LEADER	Peace be with you, Christian people,
	ALL	*amahoro.*		ALL	peace be with you.
		Amahoro kwa Yesu,			Peace be with you through Jesus,
		amahoro hallolujah!			peace be with you – hallelujah!
2	LEADER	*Urekundo, benedata*	2	LEADER	Love be with you, Christian people,
	ALL	*urekundo . . .*		ALL	love be with you . . .
3	LEADER	*Munezero, benedata*	3	LEADER	Joy be with you, Christian people,
	ALL	*munezero . . .*		ALL	joy be with you . . .

A song suitable for the exchanging of the peace. Like so many African songs, it is unaccompanied and has a leader-response format. The response could be harmonized simply.

4 AMEN, SIAKUDUMISA!

Amen, we praise your name, O God

SOUTH AFRICA

Words: unknown
Music: attributed to S. C. Molefe,
as taught by George Mxadana
arranged Dave Dargie

At a steady pace ♩ = 120
Capo 3(D)
F (D)
C (A)
LEADER
Ma - si thi!
Sing prai - ses!
Ma - si thi!
Sing prai - ses!
S. A.
A-men, si - a - ku - du - mi - sa!
A-men, we praise your name, O God!
T. B.
DESCANT
A-men, si - a - ku - du - mi - sa!
A-men, we praise your name, O God!
ECHO
A-men, si - a - ku - du - mi - sa!
A-men, we praise your name, O God!
ECHO

This exuberant song of praise was written by S. C. Molefe at a workshop in South Africa. The harmonies are rich and the 'masithi' from the leader is an encouragement to the congregation. It is very effective in procession, either at the start or at the end of a service.

Gm (Em)
F (D)
Ma - si thi!
Sing prai - ses!
A-men, si - a - ku - du - mi - sa!
A men, we praise your name, O God!
A-men, ba-wo.
A-men, a-men.
A-men, si - a - ku - du - mi - sa!
A men, we praise your name, O God!
A-men, ba-wo, A-men.
A-men, a-men, a-men.
A-men, si - a - ku - du - mi - sa!
A-men, we praise your name, O God!
A-men, ba-wo.
A-men, a-men.
Bb (G)
F/C (D)
C7 (A7)
F (D)
Ma - si thi!
Sing prai - ses!
A-men, ba - wo.
A-men, a-men.
A-men, si - a - ku - du - mi - sa!
A-men, we praise your name, O God!
A-men, A - men, ba-wo.
A-men, a - men, a-men.
A-men, si - a - ku - du - mi - sa!
A-men, we praise your name, O God!
A-men, A - men, ba-wo.
A-men, a - men, a-men.
A-men, si - a - ku - du - mi - sa!
A-men, we praise your name, O God!
A-men, A-men, ba-wo.
A-men, a-men, a-men.

5 AHSANTE YESU

We thank you, Jesus

TANZANIA

Words and music: unknown
arranged Geoff Weaver

Simply ♩ = 100
Capo 3(D)
F (D)
C7 (A7)
Ah - san - te Ye - su, a - min, Ah - san - te Ye - su, a -
We thank you, Je - sus; a - men, we thank you, Je - sus; a -
F (D)
F7 (D7)
B♭ (G)
B♭m (Gm)
F/C (D)
C7 (A7)
F (D)
- min, Ah - san - te Ye - su, a - min. Hal - le - lu - jah! A - min.
- men, we thank you, Je - sus; a - men. Hal - le - lu - jah! A - men.

Ahsante Yesu, amin,
Ahsante Yesu, amin,
Ahsante Yesu, amin.
Hallelujah! Amin.

We thank you, Jesus; amen,
we thank you, Jesus; amen,
we thank you, Jesus; amen.
Hallelujah! Amen.

A song of thanksgiving, which should be sung with simplicity and gentleness. One of the gifts of African Christians, often from poor countries like Tanzania, is their ability to give thanks in all circumstances.

6 BANI NGYETI BA YAWE

Let us praise the Lord our God

CAMEROON

Words: unknown
Music: unknown
arranged Geoff Weaver

Lively ♩ = 104
G Am D7 G
Ba - ni ngye - ti Ba Ya - we ba - ni ngye - ti Ba Ya - we
Let us praise the Lord our God, let us praise the Lord our God,

G/B C D7 G D
ba - ni ngye - ti Ba Ya - we. A - men. Hal - le - lu-yah,
let us praise the Lord our God. A - men. Hal - le - lu-jah,
Hal - le - lu-yah,
Hal - le - lu-jah,

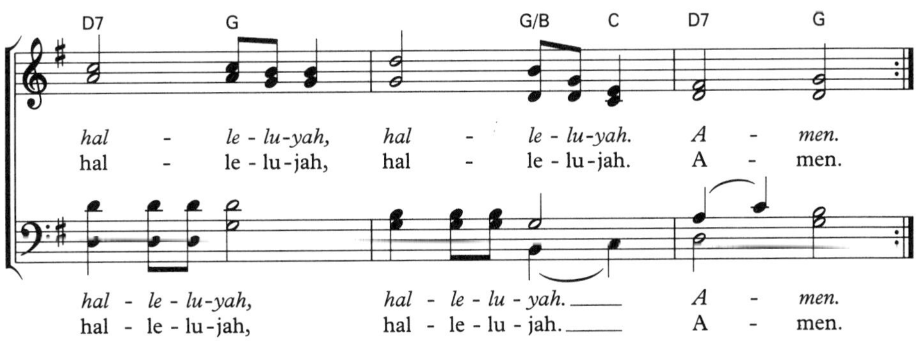
D7 G G/B C D7 G
hal - le - lu-yah, hal - le - lu-yah. A - men.
hal - le - lu-jah, hal - le - lu-jah. A - men.
hal - le - lu-yah, hal - le - lu - yah. A - men.
hal - le - lu-jah, hal - le - lu - jah. A - men.

Bani ngyeti Ba Yawe
bani ngyeti Ba Yawe
bani ngyeti Ba Yawe.
Amen.

Halleluyah, halleluyah,
halleluyah. Amen.

Let us praise the Lord our God,
let us praise the Lord our God,
let us praise the Lord our God.
Amen.

Hallelujah, hallelujah,
hallelujah. Amen.

A joyful West African song which lends itself well to added descants, rhythms and verses and indeed dance. Freedom and exuberance are the watchwords here.

7 BLESS THE LORD

KENYA

Words and music: unknown

Joyfully

LEADER
1 My sis-ters,
F C7 F
my sis-ters,
Gm F C
my sis-ters,
ALL Bless the Lord,
bless the Lord,
F C7 Dm Gm F/C C7 F
2 My bro-thers,
bless the Lord: there is no oth - er God.

ALL Bless the Lord, bless the Lord,
bless the Lord: there is no other God.

LEADER My sisters . . .

My brothers . . .

You children . . .

You elders . . .

Together . . .

A great gathering song which calls people into worship. As with many similar songs from Africa, particular groups within the congregation are addressed by the leader and may respond by singing louder in reply. The leader may wish to add other 'calls' appropriate to the community. The song should be taught without music and (if sung in harmony) in this order: SBTA.

8 BY THE BABYLONIAN RIVERS

LATVIA

Words: from Psalm 137
Ewald Bash
Music: Latvian melody
arranged Geoff Weaver

With expression ♩ = 80

Capo 3(D)

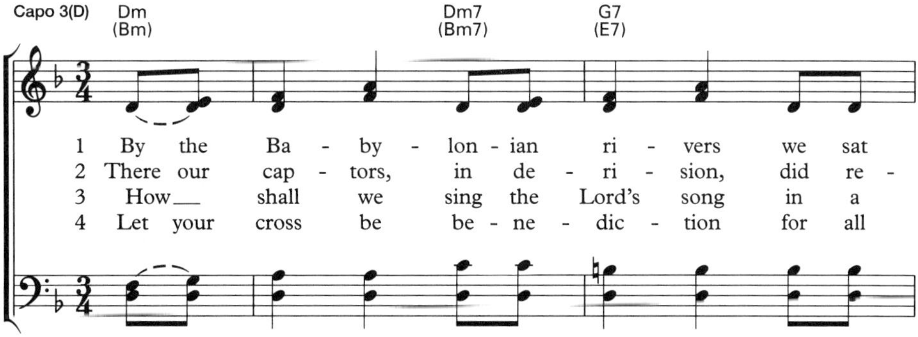

Dm (Bm)
Dm7 (Bm7)
G7 (E7)
1 By the Ba - by - lon - ian ri - vers we sat
2 There our cap - tors, in de - ri - sion, did re -
3 How__ shall we sing the Lord's song in a
4 Let your cross be be - ne - dic - tion for all

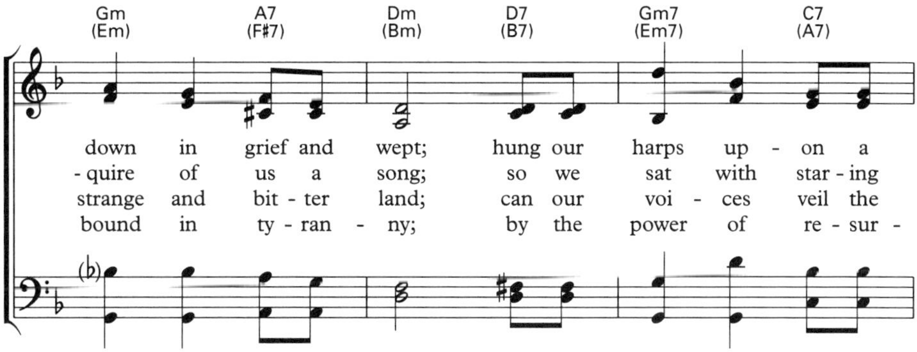

Gm (Em)
A7 (F#7)
Dm (Bm)
D7 (B7)
Gm7 (Em7)
C7 (A7)
down in grief and wept; hung our harps up - on a
-quire of us a song; so we sat with star - ing
strange and bit - ter land; can our voi - ces veil the
bound in ty - ran - ny; by the power of re - sur -

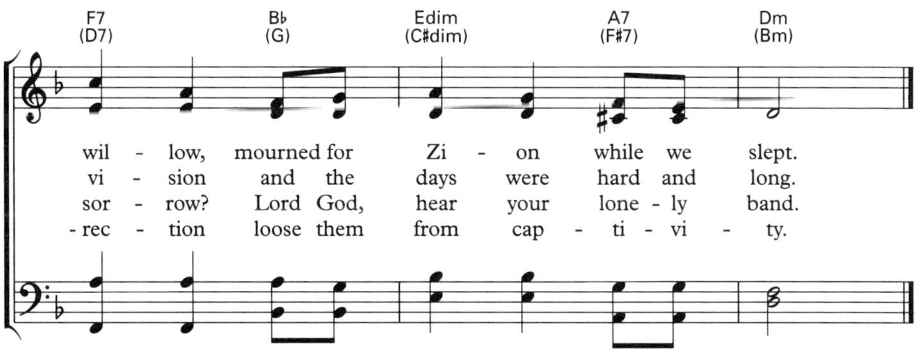

F7 (D7)
B♭ (G)
Edim (C#dim)
A7 (F#7)
Dm (Bm)
wil - low, mourned for Zi - on while we slept.
vi - sion and the days were hard and long.
sor - row? Lord God, hear your lone - ly band.
-rec - tion loose them from cap - ti - vi - ty.

This melancholy Latvian folk melody reflects beautifully the desolation of the exiles. This is very effective when sung unaccompanied or with simple guitar accompaniment.

9 BY THE WATERS OF BABYLON

Israel

Words: from Psalm 137
Music: Israeli folk melody
arranged Geoff Weaver

Flowing ♩ = 112
1
Bm A G F# Bm
By ___ the wa - ters, the wa - ters of Ba - by - lon,
2
A G F# Bm
we sat down and wept, _ and wept _ for you, Zi - on;
3
A G F# Bm
we re-mem-ber, we re-mem-ber, we re-mem-ber you, Zi - on.

The source of this very effective canon is uncertain. As with all canons, ensure that it is well known before dividing the congregation.

10 CUANDO SE VA LA ESPERANZA

Just when our hope was defeated

PERU AND COSTA RICA

Words: Ester Camac
English translation: Bret Hesla and Bill Dexheimer Pharris
Music: Edwin Mora Guevara

Am
Dm
E
Am
A
Dm
E
Am
Am
Dm
G
Cuan - do se va la es - pe - ran - za, Dios nos hab - la y nos
Just when our hope was de - feat - ed clear was the voice of the

C
Dm
Am
di - ce;
1 'Mi-ra a tu her-ma-no que vi-ve y lu-cha bus-
2 'A-cér-ca-te a tu her-ma-no y tra-ba-jen
3 'No se a-le-jen de mi la-do, per-ma-nez-can
Spi-rit:
1 'See how your bro-thers have not giv-en up in the
2 'Reach out to all of your bro-thers and build with each
3 'I will be with you and I will up-lift you and
E7
Am
Dm
-can-do un mun-do me-jor. Mi-ra a tu her-ma-na
jun-tos bus-can-do la paz. A-cér-ca-te a tu her-
fir-mes, que siem-pre es-ta-ré. No se a-le-jen de mi
strug-gle to bet-ter the world. See how your sis-ters have
oth-er a world of peace. Reach out to all of your
give you the strength to en-dure. I will be with you and
Am
E7
A
que vi-ve y lu-cha bus-can-do un mun-do me-jor.'
-ma-na y tra-ba-jen jun-tos bus-can-do la paz.'
la-do, per-ma-nez-can fir-mes, que siem-pre es-ta-ré.'
not giv-en up in the strug-gle to bet-ter the world.'
sis-ters and build with each oth-er a world of peace.'
I will up-lift you and give you the strength to en-dure.'

Chorus
A
E7
Can-te-mos a nues-tro Di-os,
el es el di-os de la
God is up-lift-ing the peo-ple.
God is the pow-er with-
A
vi-da,
Por-que el es-ta con
-in us.
Hope is our mu-sic and
E
E7
A
no-so-tros cre-an-do la es-per-an-za y la li-ber-tad!
free-dom our song and to-geth-er our voi-ces will ring.

11 CANTAI AO SENHOR

O sing to the Lord

BRAZIL

Words: anonymous
translated Gerhard Cartford
Music: Brazilian folksong
arranged Christopher Norton

Brightly 𝅗𝅥. = 70

Am Em/B B7 Em
1 Can -
1 O
Em B7
- tai ao Sen - hor um cân - ti - co no - vo, can -
(2) - que el - e fez, el - e faz mar - avil - has, por -
sing to the Lord, O sing God a new song, O
(2) God is the Lord and God has done won - ders, for
Em
- tai ao Sen - hor um cân - ti - co no - vo, can - tai ao Sen -
- que el - e fez, el - e faz mar - avil - has, por - que el - e
sing to the Lord, O sing God a new song; O sing to the
God is the Lord and God has done won-ders; for God is the
E7 Am Em/B
- hor um cân - ti - co no - vo, can - tai ao Sen - hor, can -
fez, el - e faz mar - avil - has, can - tai ao Sen - hor, can -
Lord, O sing God a new song – O sing to our God, O
Lord and God has done won-ders – O sing to our God, O

A lively Brazilian worship song that can be enhanced by a range of percussive sounds and joyful dancing.

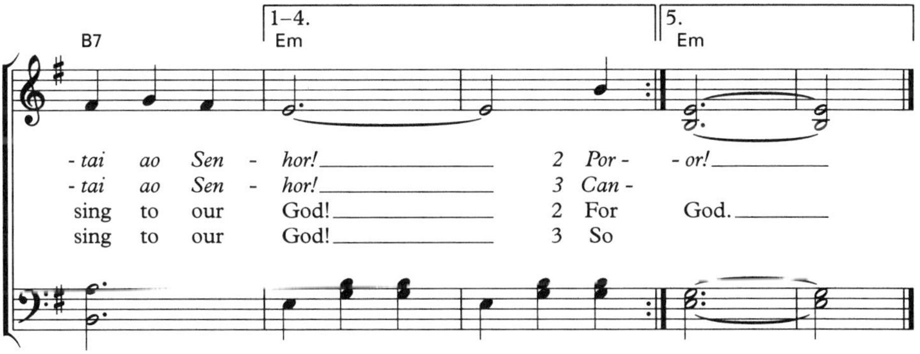

1 *Cantai ao Senhor um cântico novo,*
cantai ao Senhor um cântico novo,
cantai ao Senhor um cântico novo,
cantai ao Senhor, cantai ao Senhor!

2 *Porque ele fez, ele faz maravilhas,*
porque ele fez, ele faz maravilhas,
porque ele fez, ele faz maravilhas,
cantai ao Senhor, cantai ao Senhor!

3 *Cantai ao Senhor, bendizei o seu nome,*
cantai ao Senhor, bendizei o seu nome,
cantai ao Senhor, bendizei o seu nome,
cantai ao Senhor, cantai ao Senhor!

4 *É ele quem dá o Espírito Santo,*
é ele quem dá o Espírito Santo,
é ele quem dá o Espírito Santo,
cantai ao Senhor, cantai ao Senhor!

5 *Jesus é o Senhor! Amén, aleluia!*
Jesus é o Senhor! Amén, aleluia!
Jesus é o Senhor! Amén, aleluia!
cantai ao Senhor, cantai ao Senhor!

1 O sing to the Lord, O sing God a new song,
O sing to the Lord, O sing God a new song;
O sing to the Lord, O sing God a new song –
O sing to our God, O sing to our God!

2 For God is the Lord and God has done wonders,
for God is the Lord and God has done wonders;
for God is the Lord and God has done wonders –
O sing to our God, O sing to our God!

3 So dance for our God and blow all the trumpets,
so dance for our God and blow all the trumpets;
so dance for our God and blow all the trumpets –
O sing to our God, O sing to our God!

4 O shout to our God, who gave us the Spirit,
O shout to our God, who gave us the Spirit;
O shout to our God, who gave us the Spirit –
O sing to our God, O sing to our God!

5 For Jesus is Lord, Amen! Alleluia!
For Jesus is Lord, Amen! Alleluia!
For Jesus is Lord, Amen! Alleluia!
O sing to our God, O sing to our God!

12 CAST YOUR BURDENS (HIYA, HIYA)

Higher, higher

EAST AFRICA

Rhythmically ♩ = 112

Words and music: Issac Balinda
arranged Geoff Weaver

D G
1 Cast your burdens on to Je-sus, for he
Cast your bur-dens on to Je-sus,
A7 D
cares for you; cast your bur-dens on to
for he cares for you; cast your bur-dens
G A7 D
Je-sus, for he cares for you. High-er,
on to Je-sus, for he cares for you.
G
high-er, high-er, high-er, high-er, high-er, high-er,
High-er, high-er, high-er, high-er, high-er,

African Christians worship in dance as readily as in song, and this rhythmic song, very popular in East Africa, almost demands some simple actions.

A7
high - er, lift Je - sus
D
high - er! High - er,
high - er, lift Je - sus high - er!
high - er, high - er,
G
high - er, high - er, high - er, high - er,
High - er, high - er,
high - er, high - er, high - er,
A7
high-er, lift Je - sus
1.
D
high-er! 2 When you're
2.3.
D
fol-low.
D.S.
high-er, lift Je - sus high-er!
fol-low.

1 Cast your burdens on to Jesus,
for he cares for you;
cast your burdens on to Jesus,
for he cares for you.
Higher, higher,
higher, higher, higher,
higher, higher, higher,
lift Jesus higher!
Higher, higher,
higher, higher, higher,
higher, higher, higher,
lift Jesus higher!

2 When you're weary, follow Jesus:
for he cares for you;
when you're weary, follow Jesus:
for he cares for you.
Follow, follow,
follow, follow, follow,
follow, follow, follow,
follow Jesus, follow!
Follow, follow,
follow, follow, follow,
follow, follow, follow,
follow Jesus, follow!

Higher, higher . . .

13 CHRIST'S IS THE WORLD IN WHICH WE MOVE

SCOTLAND

A TOUCHING PLACE

Words: John L. Bell
and Graham Maule
Music: 'Dream Angus'
arranged John L. Bell
and Graham Maule

♩ = 138 (𝅗𝅥. = 46)
1 Christ's is the world_ in which we move, Christ's are the
2 Feel for the peo - ple we most a - void – strange or be -
3 Feel for the pa - rents who've lost their child, feel for the
4 Feel for the lives_ by life con - fused, rid - dled with
folk_ we're sum-moned to love, Christ's is the voice_ which
- reaved or ne - ver em - ployed; feel for the wo - men and
wo - men whom men have de - filed, feel for the ba - by for
doubt, in lov - ing ab - used; feel for the lone - ly heart,
calls us to care,_ and Christ is the one_ who meets us
feel for the men_ who fear that their liv - ing is all in
whom there's no breast and feel for the wea - ry who find no
con - scious of sin,_ which longs to be pure but fears to be -
here.
vain.
rest.
- gin.
To the lost Christ shows his face;

'A Touching Place' from the *Love from Below* collection

This song is frequently used at healing services as people come forward to have hands laid on them. Then, or at other times, it is best suited to one solo voice singing the verses and all joining in the chorus.

to the un - loved he gives his em - brace;
to those who cry in pain or dis - grace Christ
makes, with his friends, a touch - ing place.

1 Christ's is the world in which we move,
Christ's are the folk we're summoned to love,
Christ's is the voice which calls us to care,
and Christ is the one who meets us here.
  To the lost Christ shows his face;
  to the unloved he gives his embrace;
  to those who cry in pain or disgrace
  Christ makes, with his friends, a touching place.

2 Feel for the people we most avoid –
strange or bereaved or never employed;
feel for the women and feel for the men
who fear that their living is all in vain.
  To the lost . . .

3 Feel for the parents who've lost their child,
feel for the women whom men have defiled,
feel for the baby for whom there's no breast
and feel for the weary who find no rest.
  To the lost . . .

4 Feel for the lives by life confused,
riddled with doubt, in loving abused;
feel for the lonely heart, conscious of sin,
which longs to be pure but fears to begin.
  To the lost . . .

14 CHU YŎ SA SŬ MI SHI NAEN MUL

My soul longs for you

KOREA

Words: from Psalm 42
Music: Geonyong Lee

Expressively ♩ = 108

PART 1
Chu yŏ sa sŭ mi shi naen mul ch'at tŭt nae nŏk si chu rŭl ch'at sŭm ni da.
My soul longs for you, O my God, as a deer longs for flow - ing streams, for flow-ing streams.
Kal kŭ p'an nae yŏng hon i sa ra ge shin chu ni mŭl ŏn che na poe o ri kka.
My soul thirsts for God, for God, the liv - ing God: when shall I come to be - hold the face of my God?
PART 2
Chu yŏ sa sŭ mi shi naen mul ch'at tŭt nae nŏk si chu rŭl ch'at sŭm ni da.
My soul longs for you, O my God, my God, longs for flow - ing streams, thirsts for my God,
Kal kŭ p'an nae yŏng hon i sa ra ge shin chu ni mŭl ŏn che na poe o ri kka.
for my God, the liv - ing God: when shall I come, shall I come, to be - hold the face of my God?

This haunting two-part setting of words from Psalm 42 is best sung unaccompanied, following the natural accents of the text. Geonyong Lee has waited and yearned for justice and re-unification in his country of Korea, and this song powerfully reflects that longing.

15 COME NOW, O PRINCE OF PEACE

KOREA

Words: Geonyong Lee;
paraphrased by Marion Pope; altered
Music: Geonyong Lee

Steadily ♩ = 104

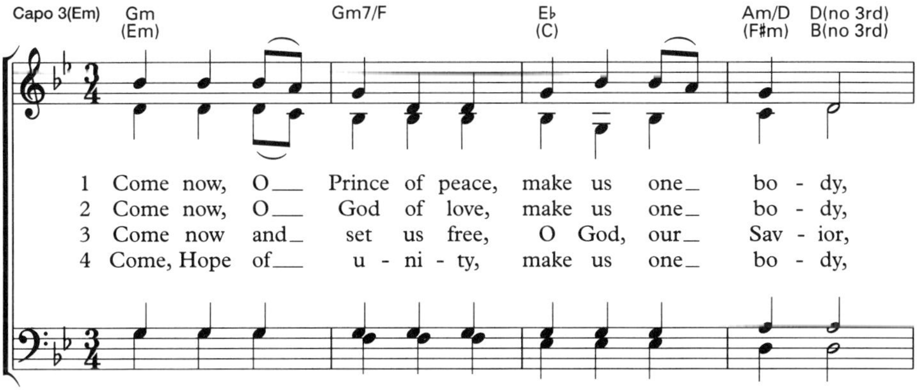

Capo 3(Em) Gm (Em) Gm7/F E♭ (C) Am/D (F♯m) D(no 3rd) B(no 3rd)
1 Come now, O Prince of peace, make us one body,
2 Come now, O God of love, make us one body,
3 Come now and set us free, O God, our Savior,
4 Come, Hope of unity, make us one body,

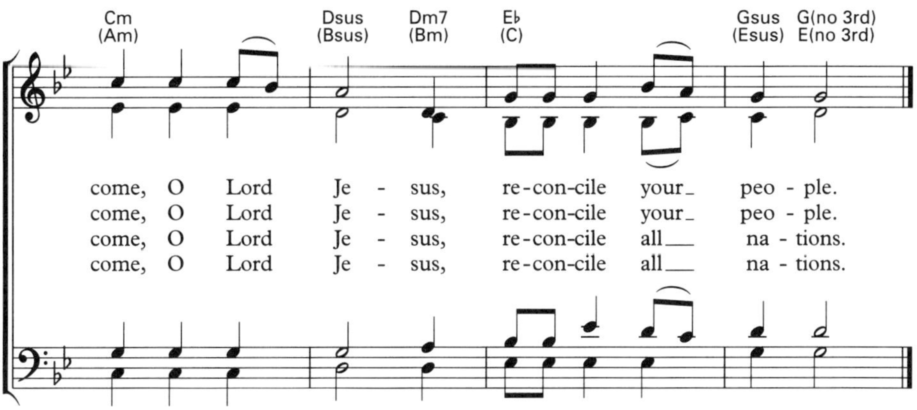

Cm (Am) Dsus (Bsus) Dm7 (Bm) E♭ (C) Gsus (Esus) G(no 3rd) E(no 3rd)
come, O Lord Jesus, reconcile your people.
come, O Lord Jesus, reconcile your people.
come, O Lord Jesus, reconcile all nations.
come, O Lord Jesus, reconcile all nations.

1 Come now, O Prince of peace,
make us one body,
come, O Lord Jesus,
reconcile your people.

2 Come now, O God of love,
make us one body,
come, O Lord Jesus,
reconcile your people.

3 Come now and set us free,
O God, our Savior,
come, O Lord Jesus,
reconcile all nations.

4 Come, Hope of unity,
make us one body,
come, O Lord Jesus,
reconcile all nations.

For most Korean Christians reunification of North and South Korea is their priority, and their urgent prayer. Geonyong Lee, one of the leading contemporary composers in Korea, has long identified himself with this struggle. Note how the dissonant harmonies paint the discord within the nation. This is very effective when sung unaccompanied.

16 COME NOW WITH JOYFUL AND THANKFUL HEARTS

INDIA

Words: from Psalm 95
James Minchin
Music: Karnatic hymn melody
arranged I-to-Loh

Rhythmically ♩ = 112
1 Come now with joy - ful and thank - ful__ hearts,
2 Know that the Lord is our might - y__ God,
3 He__ has cre - a - ted the deep blue__ sea,
in - to the courts of the King of__ kings;
ru - ler su-preme in the realms a - bove;
his own__ hands made the beau - ti - ful land;
come now with joy - ful and thank - ful__ hearts,
know that the Lord is our might - y__ God,
he__ has cre - a - ted the deep blue__ sea,
in - to the courts of the King of__ kings.
ru - ler su-preme in the realms a - bove.
his own__ hands made the beau - ti - ful land.

The Karnatic repertoire, from India, is a rich and living resource. Over a drone and repeated rhythm (perhaps played on the tambour) the melody should be strongly rhythmic.

Come and re - joice in his won - drous works –
He is the Lord of the depths be - low,
Gen - tle and kind, the Good Shep - herd he –
thank him and praise him with joy - ful psalms.
he is the strength of the moun - tains high.
we are the sheep of his pas - ture - land.
Come now with joy - ful and thank - ful hearts
in - to the courts of the King of kings.

4 Come, let us bow down and worship him,
kneel in the presence of our great God;
come, let us bow down and worship him,
kneel in the presence of our great God.
If you will listen and heed his word,
you shall be glad and your heart rejoice.
Come now with . . .

5 Glory to Father and glory to Son,
glory to Spirit and Three-in-One;
glory to Father and glory to Son,
glory to Spirit and Three-in-One.
Glory to God when the worlds began,
glory to him evermore shall be!
Come now with . . .

17 DÄR GUDS ANDE ÄR

Where the Spirit is

SWEDEN

Words and music: Jonas Jonson
arranged Geoff Weaver

Strong rhythmic 𝅗𝅥. = 76

Chorus
D C D C D
Där Guds An - de är, är fri - het.
Where the Spi - rit is, there's free - dom;
Last time to Coda
C D C D C
Där Guds An - de
where the Spi - rit
D C A7sus A7
är, där är liv.
is, there is life!
Verse
D F#m Em7 A7 D
1 In - te av värl - den kan fri - he - ten nä - ras. In - te av
2 Så - ren kan lä - kas mas - ker - na fall - er män - ska av
3 Him - mel på jor - den här får vi le - va, äl - ska och
1 Not by the world can our free - dom be nour - ished, not just by
2 Wounds will be healed, eyes will be o - pened – im - ag - ing
3 Spi - rit of God, be pres - ent a - mong us, give to us

A joyful song of freedom in the Spirit from one of Sweden's most prolific contemporary hymn writers. This needs to move, one in a bar, with great rhythmic drive.

F♯m C D F♯m
ting en - dast av An - de. Ö - va er barn att
Gud avs - peg - lar Kris - tus. Ö - va er barn att
ge bur - na av glä - dje. Ö - va er barn att
things, but by God's Spi - rit. Be sure, my child-ren, to
God, re - flect - ing Je - sus. Be sure, my child-ren, to
all strength for the jour - ney. Be sure, my child-ren, to
Em7 A7 D F♯m C
le - va i An - den läm - na er roll klä
le - va i An - den him - len är här e -
le - va i An - den vä - ga id - ag sma -
live by the Spi - rit, drop all your masks, take
live by the Spi - rit – hea - ven is here, time
live by the Spi - rit, tast - ing to - day hope
A7sus A7 D.C.
er i fri - het!
- vig i ti - den.
- ka Guds fram - tid.
free - dom's cloth - ing!
made e - ter - nal!
of God's fu - ture!
CODA
D Am7 D Am7 D
är, där är liv, där är liv.
is, there is life, there is life!

18 EL CIELO CANTA ALEGRÍA

Heaven is singing for joy

ARGENTINA

Words and music: Pablo D. Sosa
arranged Geoff Weaver

With joy and movement ♩ = 112
Bm G A D
1 El cie-lo can-ta a-le - grí - a, ¡A - le - lu - ya!
2 El cie-lo can-ta a-le - grí - a, ¡A - le - lu - ya!
1 Hea-ven is sing-ing for joy. Al - le - lu - ia!
2 Hea-ven is sing-ing for joy. Al - le - lu - ia!
Bm G F#7 Bm
por-que en tu vi-da y la mí - a bri - lla la glo - ria de Dios.
por-que a tu vi-da y la mí - a las une el a - mor de Dios.
For in your life and mine is shin-ing the glo - ry of God.
For your life and mine are one in the love of God.
A7 D A7 D
¡A - le - lu - ya, a - le - lu - ya,
Al - le - lu - ia, al - le - lu - ia,

Pablo Sosa is one of the most prolific of Argentinian hymn and songwriters, and this joyful dance song should be sung with rhythm and with abandon! A percussion accompaniment helps to highlight its dance-like character.

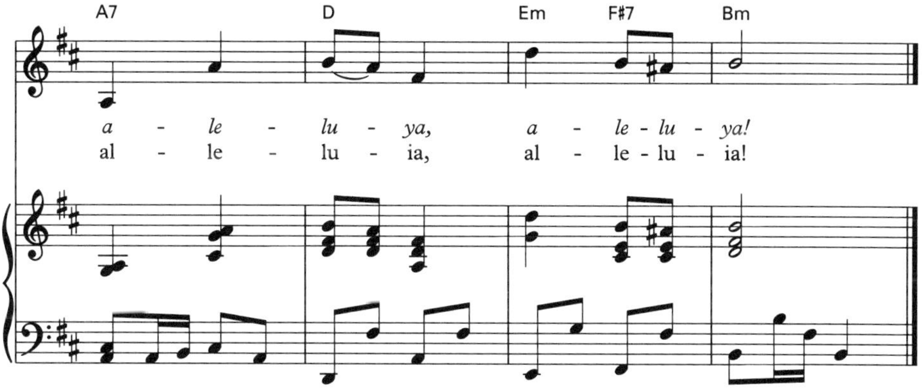
A7 D Em F#7 Bm
a - le - lu - ya, a - le - lu - ya!
al - le - lu - ia, al - le - lu - ia!

1 *El cielo canta alegría, ¡Aleluya!*
porque en tu vida y la mía brilla la gloria de Dios.
¡Aleluya, aleluya, aleluya, aleluya!

2 *El cielo canta alegría, ¡Aleluya!*
porque a tu vida y la mía las une el amor de Dios.
¡Aleluya, aleluya, aleluya, aleluya!

3 *El cielo canta alegría, ¡Aleluya!*
porque a tu vida y la mía proclamarán al Señor.
¡Aleluya, aleluya, aleluya, aleluya!

1 Heaven is singing for joy. Alleluia!
For in your life and mine is shining the glory of God.
Alleluia, alleluia, alleluia, alleluia!

2 Heaven is singing for joy. Alleluia!
For your life and mine are one in the love of God.
Alleluia, alleluia, alleluia, alleluia!

3 Heaven is singing for joy. Alleluia!
For your life and mine will always proclaim the Lord.
Alleluia, alleluia, alleluia, alleluia!

19 EL SEÑOR ÉS LA MEVA FORÇA

In the Lord I'll be ever thankful

FRANCE

Words: Taizé
Music: Jacques Berthier

♩ = 69
Capo 3(D) Dm (Bm) C (A) F (D) B♭ (G) C (A) Dm (Bm) C (A) F (D)
El Se - ñor és la me - va for - ça, el Se - ñor el me - u
In the Lord I'll be ev - er thank - ful, in the Lord I will re -
C (A) B♭ (G) A (F#) Dm (Bm) C (A)
cant. Ell m'ha e - stat la sal - va - ci - ó. En ell con -
- joice. Trust in God, do not be a - fraid. Our hearts un -
F (D) B♭ (G) C (A) Am (F#m) Dm (Bm) B♭ (G) C (A) F (D)
- fi - o, i no tinc por. En ell con - fi - o, i no tinc por.
- trou - bled, the Lord is near, our hearts un - trou - bled, the Lord is near.

Dm (Bm) C (A) F (D) B♭ (G) C (A) Dm (Bm) C (A) F (D)
El Se - ñor és la me - va for - ça, el Se - ñor el me - u
In the Lord I'll be ev - er thank - ful, in the Lord I will re -
C (A) B♭ (G) A (F♯) Dm (Bm) C (A)
cant. Ell m'ha e - stat la sal - va - ci - ó. En ell con -
- joice. Trust in God, do not be a - fraid. Our hearts un -
Fine
F (D) B♭ (G) C (A) Am (F♯m) Dm (Bm) B♭ (G) C (A) F (D) Dm (Bm) C (A)
- fi - o, i no tinc por. En ell con - fi - o, i no tinc por. El Se -
- trou-bled, the Lord is near, our hearts un - trou-bled, the Lord is near. In the

El Señor és la meva força,
el Señor el meu cant.
Ell m'ha estat
la salvació.
En ell confio,
i no tinc por.
En ell confio,
i no tinc por.

In the Lord I'll be ever thankful,
in the Lord I will rejoice.
Trust in God,
do not be afraid.
Our hearts untroubled,
the Lord is near,
our hearts untroubled,
the Lord is near.

20 ENTONEMOS UN CANTO DE ALABANZA

Let us sing to the Lord a song of praise

GUATEMALA

Words: unknown
translated G. Lockwood
in this version Word & Music
Music: Alfredo Colom
arranged Christopher Norton

Lively ♩ = 125
Em B7
1 En-to - ne-mos un can-to de a-la - ban-za en-to - ne-mos un cán-ti-co al Se-
1 Let us sing to the Lord a song of praise, let us raise all our voi-ces to the
Em E7 Am
- ñor en-to - ne - mos sal-mo-dias ce - les - tia - les en - to -
Lord, let us sing psalms of glo - ry to the Sa - vior, let us
B7 Em E7
- ne - mos mil cán - ti - cos de a - mor; en-to - ne - mos sal-mo-dias ce - les-
join in a thou-sand songs of love; let us sing psalms of glo - ry to the
Am B7 Em
- tia - les en - to - ne - mos mil cán - ti - cos de a-mor.
Sa - vior, let us join in a thou-sand songs of love.

A lively dance song which seems to cry out for guitars and light percussion accompaniment. Don't be afraid to experiment with descants and harmonies.

1 *Entonemos un canto de alabanza*
entonemos un cántico al Señor
entonemos salmodias celestiales
entonemos mil cánticos de amor;
entonemos salmodias . . .

2 *Demos gracias al Padre por la vida,*
demos gracias al Padre por Jesús.
Y sigamos la senda de la gloria
con la carga divina de la cruz;
y sigamos la senda . . .

3 *Demos gloria al Señor por este día*
por sus muchos cuidados, por su amor
porque Dios en su gran misericordia
nos dio vida en Jesús nuestro Señor;
porque Dios . . .

1 Let us sing to the Lord a song of praise,
let us raise all our voices to the Lord,
let us sing psalms of glory to the Savior,
let us join in a thousand songs of love;
let us sing psalms of glory . . .

2 Thanks we give for the gift of life you grant us,
thanks we give to our God for Jesus Christ –
so let's follow the path that leads to glory,
with the glorious burden of the cross;
so let's follow . . .

3 Let us take to ourselves the heavenly armor,
let us use all love's weapons in our cause;
we will fight for the right, till in the future
we can say, 'We are more than conquerors!'
we will fight . . .

4 Glory give to our God for each new morning,
for his wonderful blessings and his love:
for our God in the goodness of his mercy
gave us life, life in Jesus Christ our Lord;
for our God . . .

21 FOOD TO PILGRIMS

KOREA

After Geonyong Lee
in this version Word & Music
Music: Geonyong Lee
arranged Geoff Weaver

Flowing ♩ = 100

Capo 5(Am) Dm (Am) G (D) Dm (Am) Am7 (Em7)
1 Food to pil-grims giv - en, strength up - on the way;
2 Streams of grace are flow - ing – life from death for me;
3 I re - ceive your bless - ing – Jes - us, king div - ine;
Dm7 (Am7) G (D) B♭ (F) Dm (Am)
bread come down from hea - ven – Christ is ours to - day!
truth and good-ness grow - ing for e - ter - ni - ty.
all your love con - fess - ing in this bread and wine.
Am (Em) Dm (Am) B♭ (F) G (D) Dm (Am) Dm7/C B♭ (F) F (C)
Feed us now, O Lord, with this ho - ly food –
Cleanse my soul, O Lord, with your pre - cious blood –
Send me out, O Lord, ho - ly, pure and good,

A haunting song, suitable for the Eucharist, from one of Korea's leading composers, Geonyong Lee. Ideally this should be sung unaccompanied.

Am/E (Em) Dm (Am) B♭ (F) Am (Em) C (G) F7 (C7)
let your king-dom come, O Lord, let your king - dom come;
let your will be done, O Lord, let your will be done;
till the world is won, O Lord, till the world is won;
B♭ (F) Dm (Am) G (D) Dm/F (Am) Gm (Dm) Dm (Am)
let your king-dom come, O Lord, let your king - dom come.
let your will be done, O Lord, let your will be done.
till the world is won, O Lord, till the world is won.

1 Food to pilgrims given,
strength upon the way;
bread come down from heaven –
Christ is ours today!
Feed us now, O Lord, with this holy food –
let your kingdom come, O Lord, let your kingdom come;
let your kingdom come, O Lord, let your kingdom come.

2 Streams of grace are flowing –
life from death for me;
truth and goodness growing
for eternity.
Cleanse my soul, O Lord, with your precious blood –
let your will be done, O Lord, let your will be done;
let your will be done, O Lord, let your will be done.

3 I receive your blessing –
Jesus, king divine;
all your love confessing
in this bread and wine.
Send me out, O Lord, holy, pure and good,
till the world is won, O Lord, till the world is won;
till the world is won, O Lord, till the world is won.

22 FOR THE BEAUTY OF THE EARTH

CHINA

MO-LI-HUA

Words: F. Sandford Pierpoint
Music: Chinese folk song
adapted I-to-Loh

Worshipfully ♩ = 80
1 For the beau-ty_ of the earth, for the beau-ty_ of the skies,
2 For the beau-ty_ of each hour of the day_ and of the night,
3 For the joy_ of_ ear and eye, for the heart and mind's de-light,
for the love which from our birth o - ver_ and a -
hill and vale, and_ tree and flower, sun and moon and_
for the my - stic_ har - mo - ny link - ing sense to_
-round us_ lies,
stars of_ light, Christ our God, to you we_ raise
sound and sight,

This lovely Chinese folk song, used by Puccini in his opera 'Turandot', is a song about flowers. It is appropriate therefore that it should be sung as a hymn of thanksgiving for God's creation. Be particularly sensitive to the ebb and flow of the phrases.

this our sac-ri-fice of praise, this our sac - ri - fice of praise.

1 For the beauty of the earth,
for the beauty of the skies,
for the love which from our birth
over and around us lies,
Christ our God, to you we raise
this our sacrifice of praise,
this our sacrifice of praise.

2 For the beauty of each hour
of the day and of the night,
hill and vale, and tree and flower,
sun and moon and stars of light,
Christ our God . . .

3 For the joy of ear and eye,
for the heart and mind's delight,
for the mystic harmony
linking sense to sound and sight,
Christ our God . . .

4 For the joy of human love,
brother, sister, parent, child,
friends on earth and friends above,
pleasures pure and undefiled,
Christ our God . . .

5 For each perfect gift divine
to our race so freely given,
joys bestowed by love's design,
flowers of earth and fruits of heaven,
Christ our God . . .

23 FATHER IN HEAVEN

PHILIPPINES

HALAD

Words: D. T. Niles
Music: Elena G. Maquiso
arranged Geoff Weaver

Unhurried ♩ = 88
Em
1 Fa-ther in hea - ven, grant to your child - ren mer - cy and
(2) - deem - er, may we re - mem - ber your gra-cious
(3) - cend - ing, whose is the bless - ing, strength for the
F#m7
B7
Em
E7
bless - ing, songs ne - ver ceas - ing; love to u -
pas - sion, your re - sur - rec - tion: wor - ship we
wea - ry, help for the nee - dy: seal - ing Christ's
Am
Em
- nite us, grace to re - deem us, Fa - ther in
bring you, praise we shall sing you, Je - sus re -
Lord - ship, bless - ing our wor - ship, Spi - rit des -
B7
1.2.
Em
3.
Em
hea - ven, Fa-ther, our God. 2 Je - sus re -
- deem - er, Je - sus, our Lord. 3 Spi - rit des -
- cend - ing, Spi - rit a - - dored.

A beautiful hymn to the Trinity based on a Filipino folk song.
The words are by D. T. Niles, the great Sri Lankan Christian leader.

24 GET TOGETHER

CARIBBEAN

Words: unknown
Music: Caribbean melody
arranged Geoff Weaver

Rhythmically ♩ = 108

D7 G Gaug C G
Get to-geth-er, get to-geth-er, get to-geth-er in the Lord. Let us
Em7 A9 D D7 G G7
all get to-geth-er in the Lord; (in the Lord) let us greet one a-no-ther as
C G/D D7 G
sis - ter and bro-ther – let us all get to-geth-er in the Lord.

An ideal song, simple and rhythmic, for the exchanging of the Peace. The editor was literally 'caught up' while singing this song at a service in Birmingham Cathedral where the predominantly black congregation welcomed Archbishop Desmond Tutu.

25 GLORY TO GOD

PERU

Words and music: unknown

Lively but not too quickly ♩ = 132

LEADER
Glo-ry to God, glo-ry to God, glo - ry in the high - est!
ALL
Glo-ry to God, glo-ry to God, glo - ry in the high - est!
To God be glo-ry for ev - er!
To God be glo-ry for ev - er!
Al-le-lu-ia! A-men! Al-le-lu-ia! A-men!
GROUP 1
GROUP 2
Al-le-lu-ia! A-men! Al-le-lu-ia! A-men! Al-le-lu-ia! A-men!

This is ideal for celebrations and for any festive occasion. There are many ways of performing the Alleluias– feel free to experiment and to extend them. The song should be rhythmic but not too quick.

Al-le-lu-ia! A-men!
GROUP 3
Al-le-lu-ia! A-men! Al-le-lu-ia! A-men! Al-le-lu-ia! A-men! Al-le-lu-ia! A-men!

LEADER	Glory to God, glory to God, glory in the highest!
ALL	Glory to God, glory to God, glory in the highest!
LEADER	To God be glory for ever!
ALL	To God be glory for ever!
LEADER	Alleluia! Amen!
GROUP 1	Alleluia! Amen!
LEADER	Alleluia! Amen!
GROUPS 1, 2	Alleluia! Amen!
LEADER	Alleluia! Amen!
GROUPS 1, 2, 3	Alleluia! Amen!
ALL	Alleluia! Amen! Alleluia! Amen!

Additional verses:

LEADER	Glory to God, glory to God, glory to Christ Jesus . . .
LEADER	Glory to God, glory to God, glory to the Spirit . . .

26 GLORY TO THE LORD OF LOVE

Ay Ay Salidumay

PHILIPPINES

Words: from Luke 1 (Magnificat), Michael Perry
Music: based on a Kalinga melody, Henry Kiley
arranged Geoff Weaver

Simply 𝅗𝅥 = 66
WOMEN
ALL (UNISON)
1 Glo - ry to the Lord of love – in your heart pro-claim his ways: for he
3 Glo - ry to the Lord of years – now and ev - er - more the same: once he
lifts the hum-ble up, and the poor shall sing his praise– so let us love the Lord!
(Ay Ay Sa - li - du - may)
vowed to A - bra - ham, still his peo - ple trust his name, so
(Ay
Verse 1
Verse 2
SOLO INSTRUMENT
ALL
2 Glo - ry to the Lord of life – he has shown his might - y
deeds: with his arm he slays the proud, with his

A pentatonic melody, based on a Filipino folksong, which seems ideal for conveying the simple trust of Mary's response. For Filipino Christians this song is not just about Mary's response. It is also about the God who 'slays the proud and lifts up the humble and the poor'. It should ideally be sung unaccompanied. In the final phrase of each verse, the Filipino may be substituted for the English.

D.C.
hand he meets our needs: so let us love the Lord!
(Ay Ay Sa - li - du - may.)

Verse 3
let us praise, so let us praise, so let us praise the Lord!
(Ay Sa - li - du - may, Sa - li - du - may, Sa - li - du - may)

1 WOMEN Glory to the Lord of love –
in your heart proclaim his ways:
ALL for he lifts the humble up,
and the poor shall sing his praise –
so let us love the Lord!
(*Ay Ay Salidumay*)

2 ALL Glory to the Lord of life –
he has shown his mighty deeds:
with his arm he slays the proud,
with his hand he meets our needs:
so let us thank the Lord!
(*Ay Ay Salidumay*)

3 WOMEN Glory to the Lord of years –
now and evermore the same:
ALL once he vowed to Abraham,
still his people trust his name,
so let us praise,
so let us praise,
so let us praise the Lord!
(*Ay Ay Salidumay*)

27 GLORIA, GLORIA

Glory to God

FRANCE

Words: traditional
Music: Jacques Berthier

CANON

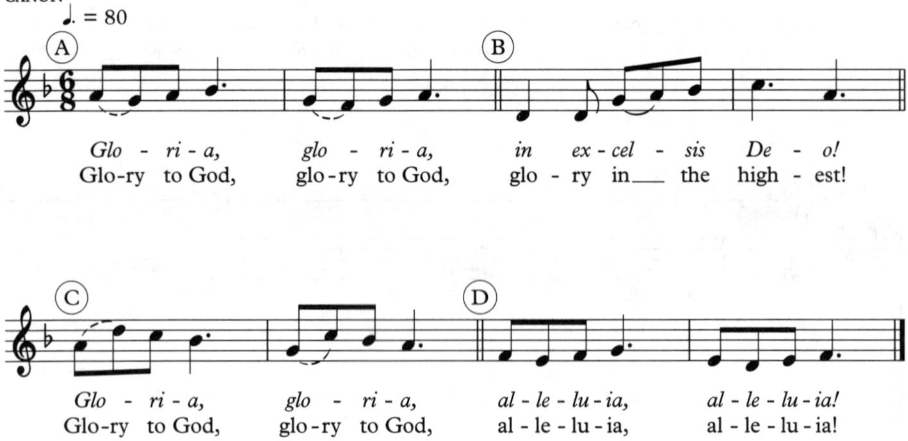
♩. = 80
A
Glo - ri - a, glo - ri - a,
Glo-ry to God, glo-ry to God,
B
in ex-cel - sis De - o!
glo - ry in the high - est!
C
Glo - ri - a, glo - ri - a,
Glo-ry to God, glo-ry to God,
D
al - le - lu-ia, al - le - lu-ia!
al - le - lu - ia, al - le - lu - ia!

KEYBOARD OR INSTRUMENTS

1 Dm Gm C F
2 Dm Gm C F
3 Dm Gm C F
4 Dm Gm C F

This item may be sung as an unaccompanied four-part canon.

28 HALLELUJAH

ZIMBABWE

Words: traditional
Music: Abraham Maraire

Dynamically 𝅗𝅥. = 66
WOMEN
Hal - le - lu - jah, hal - le - lu - jah,
TENORS
Hal - le - lu - jah, hal - le - lu -,
BASSES
Hal - le - lu - jah, hal - le - lu - jah,
hal - le - lu - jah, hal - le - lu - jah!
hal - le - lu - jah, hal - le - lu - jah!
hal - le - lu - jah, hal - le - lu - jah!

An exuberant outburst, ideal as a congregational response before and after the Gospel reading. It moves quickly, effectively one beat to a bar.

29 HALELUYA! PELO TSA RONA

Alleluia! We sing your praises

SOUTH AFRICA

Words: African origin
collected and edited by Anders Nyberg
Music: African melody
scored by Notman KB, Ljungsbro
and Lars Parkman

Confidently ♩ = 120

Chorus
Am G C G D Am
Ha - le - lu-ya! Pe - lo tsa ro - na, di tha - bi - le ka - o - fe -
Al - le - lu-ia! We sing your prais-es, all our hearts are filled with glad -

Fine
G G7 Am G/D Em D7 G
-la. Ha-le - lu-ya! Pe - lo tsa ro - na, di tha - bi - le ka - o - fe - la.
- ness. Al - le - lu-ia! We sing your prais-es, all our hearts are filled with glad-ness.

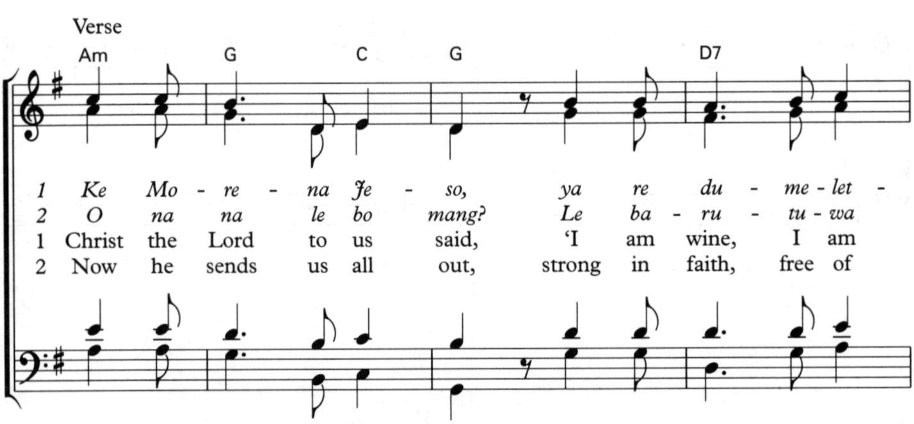
Verse
Am G C G D7
1 Ke Mo - re - na Je - so, ya re du - me - let -
2 O na na le bo mang? Le ba - ru - tu - wa
1 Christ the Lord to us said, 'I am wine, I am
2 Now he sends us all out, strong in faith, free of

An astonishing wealth of song has come out of South Africa in recent years. Songs of pain and protest, but also songs of faith and hope such as this one. The syncopated rhythms should be strongly marked.

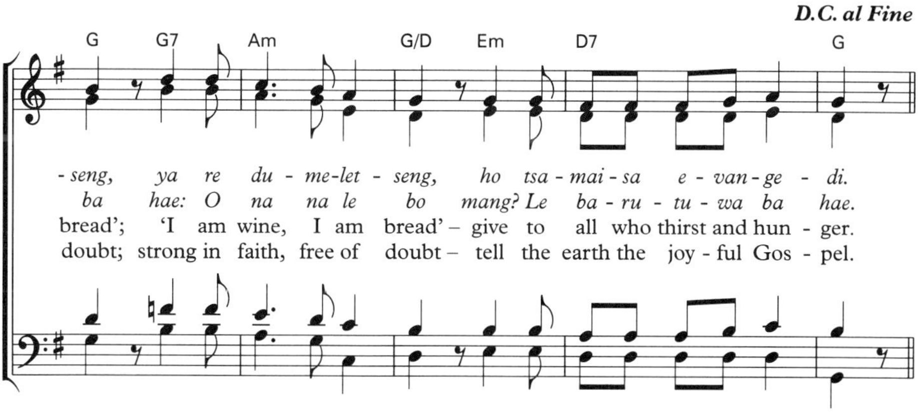
D.C. al Fine
G G7 Am G/D Em D7 G
- seng, ya re du - me-let - seng, ho tsa - mai - sa e - van - ge - di.
ba hae: O na na le bo mang? Le ba - ru - tu - wa ba hae.
bread'; 'I am wine, I am bread' – give to all who thirst and hun - ger.
doubt; strong in faith, free of doubt – tell the earth the joy - ful Gos - pel.

Haleluya! Pelo tsa rona,
di thabile kaofela.
Haleluya . . .

1 *Ke Morena Jeso,*
ya re dumeletseng,
ya re dumeletseng,
ho tsamaisa evangedi.
Haleluya . . .

2 *O na na le bo mang?*
Le barutuwa ba hae:
O na na le bo mang?
Le barutuwa ba hae.
Haleluya . . .

Alleluia!
We sing your praises,
all our hearts
are filled with gladness.
Alleluia . . .

1 Christ the Lord to us said,
'I am wine, I am bread';
'I am wine, I am bread' –
give to all who thirst and hunger.
Alleluia . . .

2 Now he sends us all out,
strong in faith, free of doubt;
strong in faith, free of doubt –
tell the earth the joyful Gospel.
Alleluia . . .

30 HALLE, HALLE, HALLELUJAH

CARIBBEAN

Words: traditional
Music: unknown
arranged Geoff Weaver

Lively ♩ = 112
G
G D/F♯ Em
Hal - le, hal - le, hal - le - lu - jah!
C
Am D
Hal - le, hal - le, hal - le - lu - jah!
hal - le - lu - jah
G
D/F♯ Em
Hal - le, hal - le, hal - le - lu - jah! Hal - le -
Am7 G/D D7 G C G/B Am7
- lu - jah, hal - le - lu - jah!
hal - le - lu - jah

A song from the Caribbean, where many people are uninhibited in expressing their worship.

G G D/F# Em
Hal - le, hal - le, hal - le - lu - jah!
C Am D
Hal - le, hal - le, hal - le - lu - jah!
hal - le - lu - jah
G D/F# Em
Hal - le, hal - le, hal - le - lu - jah! Hal - le -
Am7 G/D D7 G
- lu - jah, hal - le - lu - jah!

31 HAVE YOU EVER SEEN

PAKISTAN

Words: Narayan Vaman Tilak (Marathi)
translated Nicol Macnicol (adapted)
Music: Urdu melody
arranged Geoff Weaver

With feeling 𝅗𝅥 = 76
Capo 1(D)
Eb (D) Cm (Bm) Fm (Em) Fm7
1 Have you ev - er seen the Lord, Christ the cru - ci - fied? Have you
2 Have you seen your-self in them – one who hurt him so? Have you
3 Have you seen how he, to save, suf - fers there and dies? Have you
Bb (A) Fm (Em) Bb7 (A7) Eb (D)
seen those wound-ed hands? Have you seen his side? Have you
seen the sin - ner who caused your sav - ior's woe? Have you
seen on whom he looks with his lov - ing eyes? Have you
Gm (F#m) Cm (Bm) Fm (Em)
seen the cru - el thorns, wo - ven for a crown? Have you,
seen the cloak of night which dark Cal - vary wore? Have you
ev - er, ev - er seen love so deep as this? Have you

A haunting Urdu song inviting the listener to contemplate the sufferings of Christ, and to respond with self-offering. Be aware of the growing intensity of the phrase through the repeated melodic notes.

Bb7 (A7) Fm (Em) Bb7 (A7) Eb (D)
have you seen his blood, drop-ping, drop-ping down? Have you
seen a lone-li-ness such as Je-sus bore? Have you
giv-en up your life whol-ly to be his? Have you
Cm (Bm) Fm (Em) Fm7
seen the cru-el thorns wo-ven for a crown? Have you,
seen the cloak of night which dark Cal-vary wore? Have you
ev-er, ev-er seen love so deep as this? Have you
Bb (A) Fm (Em) Bb7 (A7) Eb (D) Bb7/Eb (A7) Eb (D)
have you seen his blood, drop-ping, drop-ping down?
seen a lone li-ness such as Je-sus bore?
giv-en up your life whol-ly to be his?

1 Have you ever seen the Lord,
Christ the crucified?
Have you seen those wounded hands?
Have you seen his side?
Have you seen the cruel thorns,
woven for a crown?
Have you, have you seen his blood,
dropping, dropping down?
Have you seen the cruel thorns . . .

2 Have you seen yourself in them –
one who hurt him so?
Have you seen the sinner who
caused your savior's woe?
Have you seen the cloak of night
which dark Calvary wore?
Have you seen a loneliness
such as Jesus bore?
Have you seen the cloak of night . . .

3 Have you seen how he, to save,
suffers there and dies?
Have you seen on whom he looks
with his loving eyes?
Have you ever, ever seen
love so deep as this?
Have you given up your life
wholly to be his?
Have you ever, ever seen . . .

32 HAY MOMENTOS

There are moments

ARGENTINA

Words: unknown
translated Dina de Carro
Music: unknown
arranged David Peacock

Steadily ♩ = 104
G/A D Dmaj7 D7 Em/G A G/A
Hay mo - men - tos, que las pa - la - bras no al - can - zan, pa - ra de - cir - te lo que sien - to por ti mi buen Se - ñor. Hay mo -
There are mo - ments when words can-not ex-press com - plete - ly all the feel - ings that my heart can hold for you my God and Lord. There are
1. 2. C/D
por tí mi buen Se - ñor. Yo te a - gra -
for you my God and Lord. And I will

A popular worship song which is used throughout Central America.

G
A7/G
F#m
- dez - co por to - do lo que hi - cis - te,
praise you for all that you have done, Lord,
Bm7
Em
por to - do lo que ha - ces,
for all that you are do - ing,
1.
A7
Dsus
D7
C/D
y to - do lo que ha-rás. Yo te a - gra -
for all that you will do. And I will
2.
A7
D
y to - do lo que ha - rás.
for all that you will do.

33 HE CAME DOWN

CAMEROON

Words and music: unknown
arranged Geoff Weaver

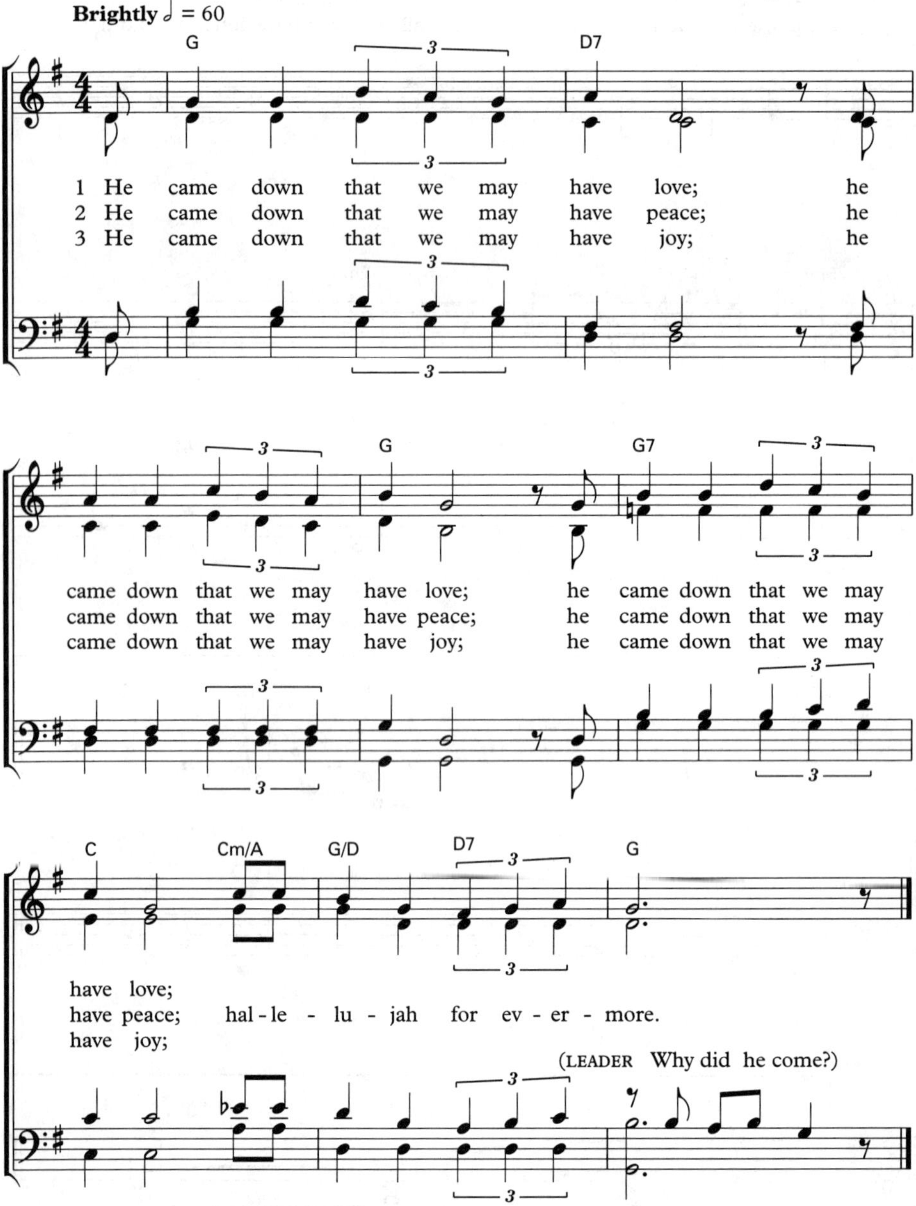
Brightly 𝅗𝅥 = 60
G
D7
1 He came down that we may have love; he
2 He came down that we may have peace; he
3 He came down that we may have joy; he
G
G7
came down that we may have love; he came down that we may
came down that we may have peace; he came down that we may
came down that we may have joy; he came down that we may
C
Cm/A
G/D
D7
G
have love;
have peace; hal-le - lu - jah for ev - er - more.
have joy;
(LEADER Why did he come?)

4 He came down that we may have power . . .

5 He came down that we may have hope . . .

A traditional Cameroonian song, which is often performed as a circle dance with sweeping movements to suggest Christ's coming down. The leader calls and encourages the congregation to respond.

34 HOSANNA, HOSANNA, HOSANNA

FRANCE

Words: traditional
Music: Jacques Berthier

CANON ♩ = 116

A B C D
Ho - san - na, ho - san - na, ho - san - na in ex - cel - sis. Ho -
Ho - san - na, ho - san - na, ho - san - na in the high - est! Ho -

ACCOMPANIMENTS

KEYBOARD

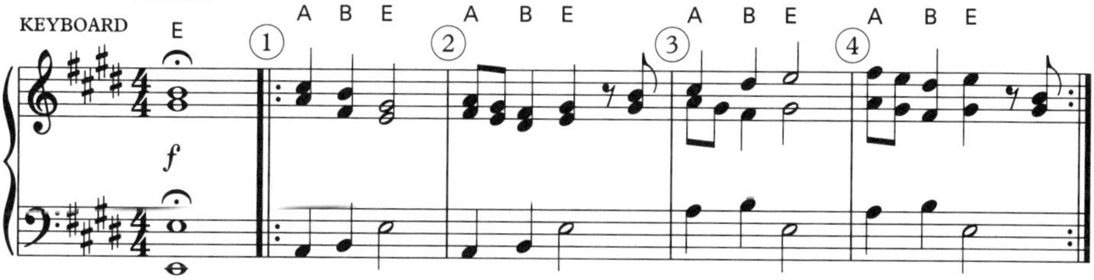
E
A B E A B E A B E A B E
1 2 3 4
f

CHOIR

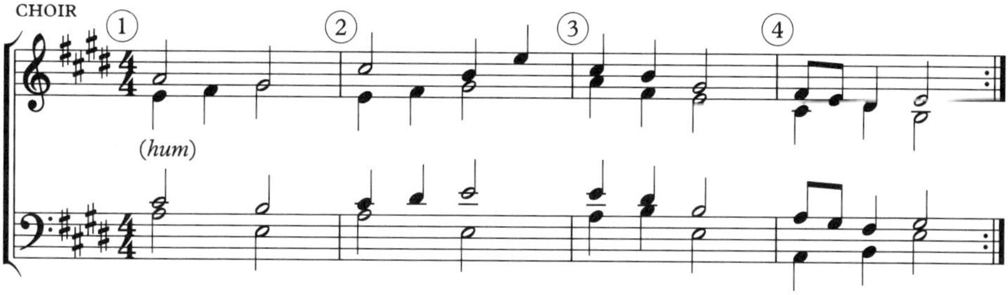
1 2 3 4
(hum)

SOPRANO OR INSTRUMENT (after the completion of the Canon)

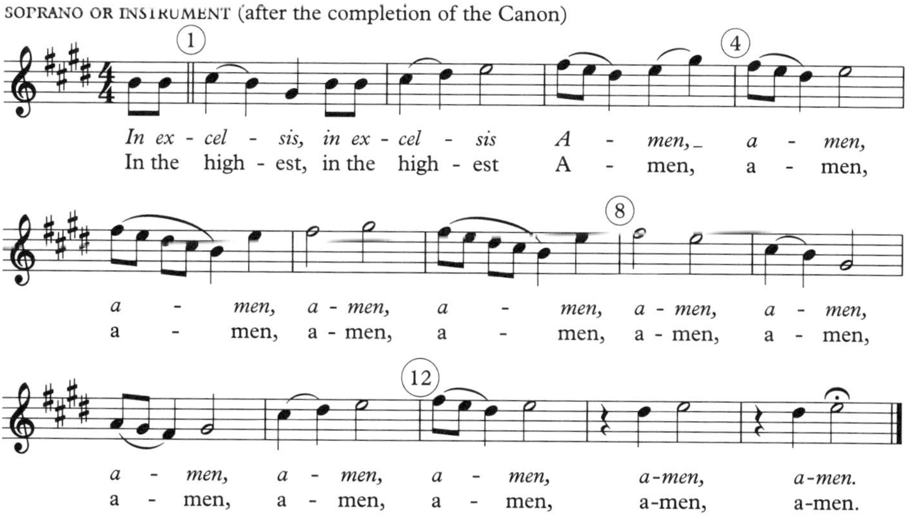
1 4
In ex - cel - sis, in ex - cel - sis A - men, a - men,
In the high - est, in the high - est A - men, a - men,
8
a - men, a - men, a - men, a - men, a - men,
a - men, a - men, a - men, a - men, a - men,
12
a - men, a - men, a - men, a-men, a-men.
a - men, a - men, a - men, a-men, a-men.

Many who have gone to Taizé have been moved by the worship, with its use of repeated chants, which touch the depths of our being. A round or canon such as this enables a congregation to create harmony, giving an added dimension to their worship.

35 HE CAME SINGING LOVE

NEW ZEALAND

Words and music: Colin Gibson

Capo 1(D)
Eb (D) Eb/D Cm (Bm)
1 He came sing-ing love and he lived sing-ing love; he
2 He came sing-ing faith and he lived sing-ing faith; he
3 He came sing-ing hope and he lived sing-ing hope; he
4 He came sing-ing peace and he lived sing-ing peace; he
Eb/G (D) Ab (G) 3 Eb (D) Bb/D (A) Cm (Bm)
died sing-ing love.
died sing-ing faith.
died sing-ing hope.
died sing-ing peace.
He a - rose in
Gm (F#m) Eb (D) Ab (G) Bb7 (A7)
si - lence. For the love faith hope peace to go on we must

1 He came singing love
and he lived singing love;
he died singing love.
He arose in silence.
For the love to go on
we must make it our song:
you and I be the singers.

2 He came singing faith
and he lived singing faith;
he died singing faith.
He arose in silence.
For the faith to go on
we must make it our song:
you and I be the singers.

3 He came singing hope
and he lived singing hope;
he died singing hope.
He arose in silence.
For the hope to go on
we must make it our song:
you and I be the singers.

4 He came singing peace
and he lived singing peace;
he died singing peace.
He arose in silence.
For the peace to go on
we must make it our song:
you and I be the singers.

36 HE IS RISEN

East Africa

Words and music: unknown
Music arranged David Peacock

Lively ♩ = 120
E B7 E
He is ris - en, ris - en, ris - en; he is
(ris-en) (ris-en) (ris-en)
B7 1. E 2. E
ris-en, ris-en – the Lord: he is Lord!
(ris-en, ris-en – the Lord: Lord!)
LEADER ALL
1 Oh be joy - ful – join in praise and sing: O al - le - lu - ia!
2 O-ver death's power Je - sus has o - ver - come: O al - le - lu - ia!
3 Al - le - lu - ia! All Christ-ians, join us now: O al - le - lu - ia!
B7
E
LEADER ALL
We were all dead; we now live in Je - sus: O
Life e - ter - nal Je - sus has giv - en us: O
He's tri - um - phant! All Christ-ians, praise him now, O

Of uncertain origin, this song has many of the hallmarks of Africa – a leader calling for a response and lively rhythms to celebrate Christ's resurrection.

1.2.
3.
B7
E
D.S.
E
al - le - lu - ia! He is
al - le - lu - ia! He is
al - le - lu - - ia! Al - le -
B7
E
- lu - ia, - lu - ia, - lu - ia; al - le -
(- lu - ia) (- lu - ia) (- lu - ia)
B7
E
B7
- lu - ia life is come: he is ris - en, ris - en,
(- lu-ia life is come:) (ris-en) (ris-en)
E
B7
E
ris - en; he is ris - en, ris - en – the Lord!
(ris-en) (ris-en: ris - en – the Lord!)

37 HEME AQUÍ

Here I am

Mexico

Words: Marcos Witt
translated Word & Music
Music: Marcos Witt
arranged David Peacock

Worshipfully ♩ = 95

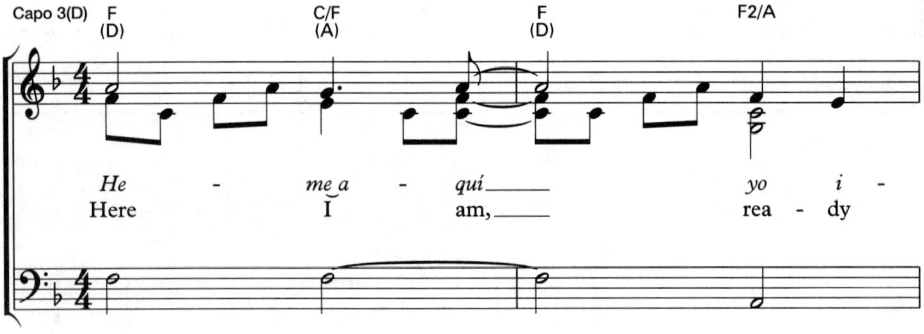

Capo 3(D)
F (D)
C/F (A)
F (D)
F2/A
He - me a - quí yo i -
Here I am, rea - dy

B♭2 (G)
C (A)
B♭/C (G)
C (A)
F (D)
C/F (A)
- ré Se - ñor; he - me a - quí
for you, Lord; here I am,

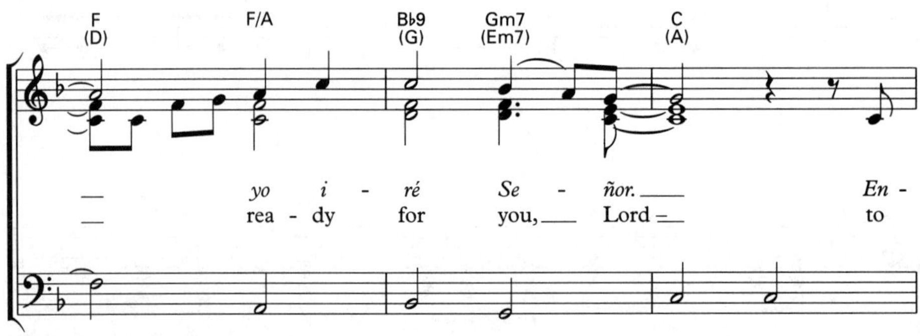

F (D)
F/A
B♭9 (G)
Gm7 (Em7)
C (A)
yo i - ré Se - ñor. En -
rea - dy for you, Lord to

Marcos Witt's songs are increasingly used throughout Latin America. This is an ideal song for times of response.

Gm7 (Em7) C (A)
-ví - a - me a mi, que dis -
go where you will send, and to
F (D) F/A B♭2 (G) B♭2/A Gm7 (Em7)
-pues - to es - toy, lle - va - ré tu Glo-
give my life to pro-claim your glo-
C (A7) C7 Gm/F (Em) F (D)
3
- ria a las na - cio - nes.
- ry to all the na - tions.

Heme aquí yo iré Señor;
heme aquí yo iré Señor.
Envíame a mi,
que dispuesto estoy,
llevaré tu Gloria a las naciones.

Here I am, ready for you, Lord;
here I am, ready for you, Lord –
to go where you will send,
and to give my life
to proclaim your glory to all the nations.

38 HUMBLY IN YOUR SIGHT

MALAWI

Words and music: Tom Colvin
arranged Geoff Weaver

Easy movement ♩ = 96

Capo 3(D)
F (D) C/E (A) F (D) C (A) Dm (Bm) Gm (Em) C (A)
1 Hum - bly in your sight we come to - ge - ther, Lord:
2 These our hearts are yours– we give them to you, Lord:
3 These our ears are yours, we give them to you, Lord:
4 These our eyes are yours, we give them to you, Lord:

F (D) C (A) Dm (Bm) Gm/B♭ (Em) C6 (A) C7 F (D)
grant us now the bless - ing of your pre - sence here.
pu - ri - fy our love to make it like your own.
o - pen them to hear the gos - pel straight from you.
may we al - ways see this world as with your sight.

Alternative setting for verses 3 and 7.
Sopranos sing the words, lower voices hum

F (D) C (A) Dm (Bm) C (A) B♭ (G) Gm7 (Em7) C7/G (A7)
3 These our ears are yours, we give them to you, Lord:
7 These our feet are yours, we give them to you, Lord:

A simple Malawian folk song with straightforward harmonies, effective when sung as people gather for worship

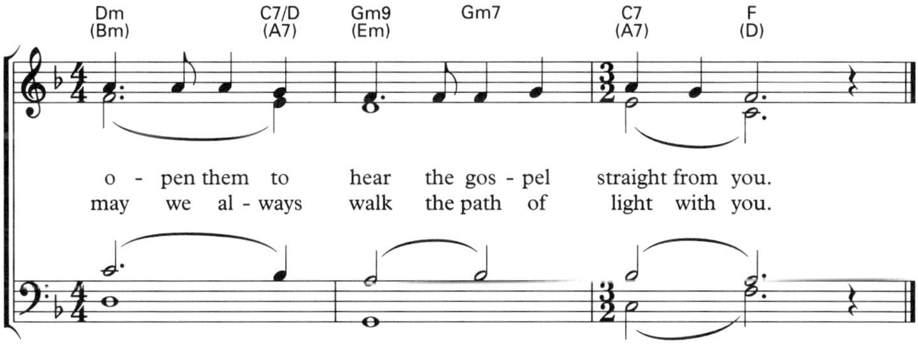
Dm (Bm) C7/D (A7) Gm9 (Em) Gm7 C7 (A7) F (D)
o - pen them to hear the gos - pel straight from you.
may we al - ways walk the path of light with you.

1 Humbly in your sight we come together, Lord:
grant us now the blessing of your presence here.

2 These our hearts are yours – we give them to you, Lord:
purify our love to make it like your own.

3 These our ears are yours, we give them to you, Lord:
open them to hear the gospel straight from you.

4 These our eyes are yours, we give them to you, Lord:
may we always see this world as with your sight.

5 These our hands are yours, we give them to you, Lord:
give them strength and skill to work and build for you.

6 These our tongues are yours, we give them to you, Lord:
may we speak your healing words of light and truth.

7 These our feet are yours, we give them to you, Lord:
may we always walk the path of light with you.

8 Our whole selves are yours, we give them to you, Lord:
take us now and keep us safe for evermore.

39 I WILL SING UNTO THE LORD

NIGERIA

Words and music: unknown
arranged Geoff Weaver

With joy and rhythmic freedom 𝅗𝅥 = 112

G
C
I will sing un - to the Lord a joy - ful song, and
Am
G/D
D7
G
bless his name for the Lord is good;
G
C
C/G G
I will sing un - to the Lord, I will sing un - to the Lord, I will

We heard this joyful song, rather reminiscent of Psalm 105 in its sentiments, sung with great verve and vitality by the Yorubas of Nigeria. Feel the rhythm rather than counting it, and don't be afraid to exercise freedom and creativity.

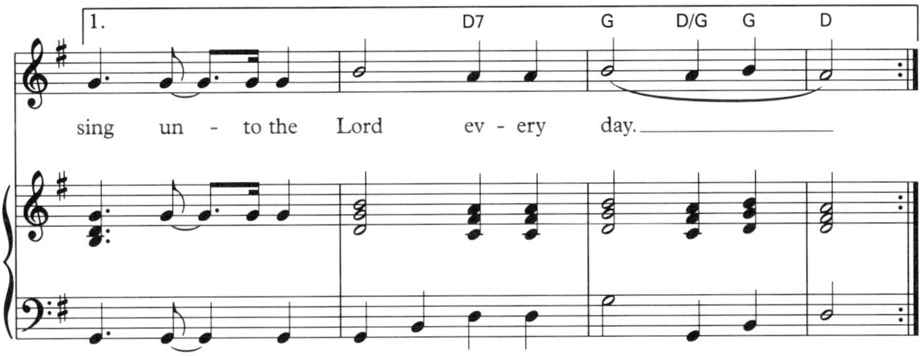
1.
D7 G D/G G D
sing un - to the Lord ev - ery day.

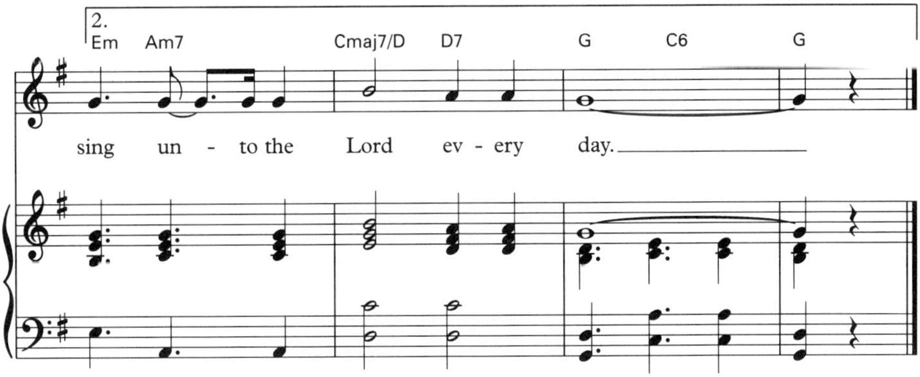
2.
Em Am7 Cmaj7/D D7 G C6 G
sing un - to the Lord ev - ery day.

I will sing unto the Lord a joyful song,
and bless his name for the Lord is good;
I will sing unto the Lord a joyful song,
and bless his name for the Lord is good.
I will sing unto the Lord,
I will sing unto the Lord,
I will sing unto the Lord every day.
I will sing unto the Lord,
I will sing unto the Lord,
I will sing unto the Lord every day.

40 ID Y PREDICAD

Go in Jesus' name

SPAIN

Words: from Luke 6, 9, 10 etc.
Josep Laporta and Ethel López
translated Word & Music
Music: Josep Laporta

Steadily ♩ = 125

C G/B Am Am7/G F G7/F
1 Id y pre - di - cad, el e - van - ge - lio
2 Id y a - nun - ciad, sa - nad las lla - gas
1 Go in Je - sus' name to spread the news of
2 Go in Je - sus' name – yes, go to set the
Em7 Am Dm7 G7 Em7 Am
de la paz; al - zad los o - jos pa - ra ver que es
del do - lor, se - cad los o - jos, con - so - lad, que el
joy and peace: the har - vest fields are rea - dy now – it's
pris - oners free, to preach the good news to the poor, to
Dm7 Gsus G C G/B
tiem - po de se - gar. Id y con - fi - ad
mun-do llo - ran - do es - tá. Id y res - tau - rad,
time to start to reap. Go – his love pro - claim:
com - fort those who weep. Go to heal the lame,

A call to action from one of Spain's notable Christian musicians. A strong rhythmic character is essential, particularly in the syncopation of the refrain. However, the song should not be taken too fast.

Am Am7/G F G7/F Em7 Am
que sus pro - me - sas cum - pli - rá; pa -
al que bran - ta - do co - ra - zón, su
his pro - mis - es will be ful - filled, and
bind up the wea - ry, bro - ken hearts; for
Dm7 G7 Em7 Am
- la - bras de gra - cia os da - rá en
gra - cia a - bun - dan - te bas - ta - rá, sus
when you are called to speak for him he'll
where you are called to work for him he'll
Dm7 Gsus G
ca - da ne - ce - si - dad.
car - gas a - li - via - rá.
give you the words to say.
give you his strength each day.
C F/C G/C F/C C
Pa - ra que el mun - do cre - a,
Let all the world be - lieve him,

F/C G/C F/C C Am7
pa - ra que el mun - do se - pa: que en él hay per - dón,
let all the world re - ceive him! In Christ there is peace,
Em7 E7/G# Am Am/G
que en él hay po - der,
in Christ there is power;
F F/G G7 C
pa - ra que el mun - do se - pa hoy.
Christ is the hope of all the world.

INSTRUMENTAL LINK AND ENDING

C F/C G/C F/C C C F/C G/C

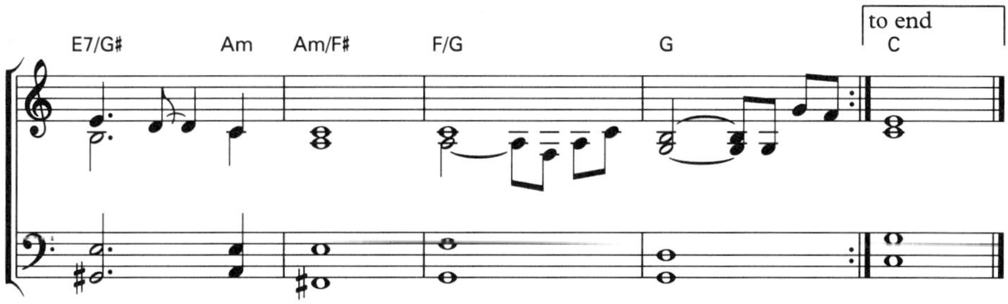

1 *Id y predicad,*
el evangelio de la paz;
alzad los ojos para ver
que es tiempo de segar.
Id y confiad
que sus promesas cumplirá;
palabras de gracia os dará
en cada necesidad.
Para que el mundo crea,
para que el mundo sepa:
que en él hay perdón,
que en él hay poder,
para que el mundo sepa hoy.

2 *Id y anunciad,*
sanad las llagas del dolor,
secad los ojos, consolad,
que el mundo llorando está.
Id y restaurad,
al que brantado corazón,
su gracia abundante bastará,
sus cargas aliviará.
Para que . . .

1 Go in Jesus' name
to spread the news of joy and peace:
the harvest fields are ready now –
it's time to start to reap.
Go – his love proclaim:
his promises will be fulfilled,
and when you are called to speak for him
he'll give you the words to say.
Let all the world believe him,
let all the world receive him!
In Christ there is peace,
in Christ there is power;
Christ is the hope of all the world.

2 Go in Jesus' name –
yes, go to set the prisoners free,
to preach the good news to the poor,
to comfort those who weep.
Go to heal the lame,
bind up the weary, broken hearts;
for where you are called to work for him
he'll give you his strength each day.
Let all the world . . .

41 IN SILENT STILLNESS

PAKISTAN

Words: from Psalm 62
translated from the Punjabi
by Alison Blenkinsop
Music: unknown
arranged Geoff Weaver

Confidently ♩. = 68
Chorus
Capo 3(Em)
Gm (Em) F/G (D) Gm (Em) F/G (D) Cm (Am) D (B)
In si - lent still-ness, wait for God and rest, my soul, in peace: in
last time to Coda
Gm (Em) F/G (D) Gm (Em) F/G (D) Cm (Am)
him your hopes will be ful-filled, your fears will find re -
Verse
D (B) Gm (Em) F/G (D) Gm (Em) Dm (Bm)
1 He is the for - tress of my soul, he is the for - tress
- lease. 2 He is my strong de - liv - er - er, he is my strong de -
3 Let all the na - tions trust in him, let all the na - tions

This expressive Punjabi setting of words from Psalm 62 is sung by Pakistani Christians who are a very small minority in an Islamic state. Although in the minor key, it should be sung with rhythm and conviction. When changing from $\frac{6}{8}$ to $\frac{8}{8}$, the speed of the dotted quarter is equal to the quarter of the new pattern.

Gm (Em) Bb (G) Cm (Am) Gm (Em)
of my soul – my Rock, my hid - ing - place, my
-liv - er - er – I'm safe with - in his hand, I'm
trust in him and bow be - fore his throne, and
Cm (Am) F (D) Bb (G)
Rock, my hid - ing - place; so I shall not be o - ver-come, de -
safe with-in his hand, the Lord is my de-fend-er and the
bow be-fore his throne, and wor-ship him with hum-ble hearts – for
Cm (Am) D (B) Gm (Em)
-feat I'll ne - ver face, so I shall not be o - ver-come, de -
rock on which I stand, the Lord is my de-fend - er and the
he is God a - lone, and wor-ship him with hum-ble hearts – for
Cm (Am) D (B)
-feat I'll ne-ver face!
rock on which I stand. In
he is God a-lone.
CODA
Cm (Am) Gm (Em)
fears will find re - lease.

42 ISA MASIH

Jesus the Lord is seeking me

PAKISTAN

Words: translated from the original
by Alison Blenkinsop
Music: unknown

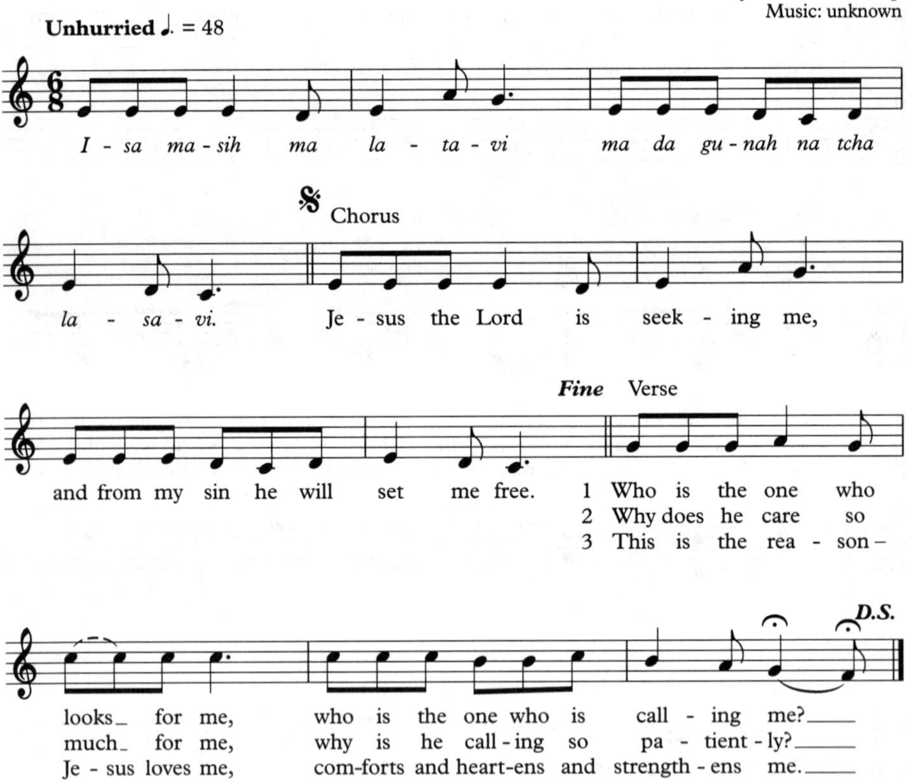
Unhurried ♩. = 48
I - sa ma - sih ma la - ta - vi ma da gu - nah na tcha
la - sa - vi.
Chorus
Je - sus the Lord is seek - ing me,
and from my sin he will set me free.
Fine
Verse
1 Who is the one who looks for me, who is the one who is call - ing me?
2 Why does he care so much for me, why is he call - ing so pa - tient - ly?
3 This is the rea - son – Je - sus loves me, com-forts and heart-ens and strength - ens me.
D.S.

4 How can he give such comfort to me –
there is such weakness and sin in me.
Jesus the Lord . . .

5 He gave his life in sacrifice
and for my sin he has paid the price.
Jesus the Lord . . .

6 I am so glad he set me free –
I'll live with God for eternity.
Jesus the Lord . . .

This haunting song comes from the North-West Frontier province of Pakistan, and is best sung unaccompanied. Christians in Pakistan are in a small minority. It is good that we remember them and identify with them as we sing this song.

43 ISHWORO

Father in heaven

INDIA

KYRIE

Words: traditional
Music: unknown
arranged Geoff Weaver

Intensely ♩ = 84
SOLO
F♯m
ALL
Ish - wo-ro, Ish - wo-ro da-ya ko-ro; Ish - wo-ro, Ish - wo-ro
Fa - ther in hea-ven, have mer-cy up-on us; Fa - ther in hea-ven, have
A/C♯
F♯m
SOLO
da-ya ko-ro. Ish - wo - ro da-ya ko-ro;
mer-cy up-on us. Je - sus Christ, have mer-cy up-on us;
F♯m/C♯
ALL
Bm
C♯m7
F♯m
SOLO
Ish - wo - ro da-ya ko-ro. Ish - wo-ro, Ish - wo-ro
Je - sus Christ, have mer-cy up-on us. Fa - ther in hea-ven, have
F♯m
ALL
rit.
C♯m7
F♯m
da-ya ko-ro; Ish - wo-ro, Ish - wo-ro da-ya ko-ro.
mer-cy up-on us; Fa - ther in hea-ven, have mer-cy up-on us.

A solo-response Kyrie eleison (Lord, have mercy), characteristically Indian in its melodic shape. It should be sung with heartfelt yearning.

44 JE LOUERAI L'ÉTERNEL

I long to praise the Lord

FRANCE

Words: from Psalm 9, Louis Segond and Y. Keler
translated Robert Atkins
Music: Claude Fraysse, harmonisation Alain Berg
arranged Geoff Weaver

Worshipfully ♩ = 88
VERSION 1

Capo 3(D)
F (D) C7 (A7) Dm (Bm) B♭ (G) C7 (A7)
1 Je loue-rai l'É - ter - nel de tout mon
1 I long to praise the Lord with all of my
F (D) F7 B♭ (G) C7 (A7) F (D) Dm (Bm)
cöur, je ra - con-te - rai tou - tes tes mer-veil - les, je
heart, in praise to be sung by each tribe and tongue I
Gm (Em) Csus (A) C7 F (D) C7 (A7) Dm (Bm) F7 (D7)
chan - te - rai ton nom. Je loue-rai l'É - ter - nel de
long to sing my part. I long to praise the Lord with
B♭ (G) C7 (A7) F (D) F7 B♭ (G) C7 (A7)
tout mon cöur, je fe - rai de toi le
all of my heart, I long to em-ploy my

A gentle song of worship from France. The two arrangements allow for either congregational or choral use.

A/C# (F#) Dm (Bm) Gm (Em) Gm/C F (D)
su - jet de ma joie, al - le - lu - ia!
voice to tell my joy. Al - le - lu - ia!
VERSION 2
F (D) B♭ (G) C7 (A7) Dm (Bm) Gm (Em) C7 (A7)
1 Je loue-rai l'É - ter - nel de tout mon
1 I long to praise the Lord with all of my
F (D) F7 B♭ (G) C7 (A7) F (D) A7 (F#) Dm (Bm)
cöur, je ra - con - te - rai tou - tes tes mer-veil - les, je
heart, in praise to be sung by each tribe and tongue I
Gm (Em) Gm/C C7 (A7) F (D) C7 (A7)
chan - te - rai ton nom. Je loue-rai l'É - ter -
long to sing my part. I long to praise the
Dm (Bm) Gm7 (Em) C7 (A7) F (D) F7 B♭ (G) C7 (A7)
- nel de tout mon cöur, je fe - rai de toi le
Lord with all of my heart, I long to em-ploy my

A/C# (F#)
Dm (Bm)
Gm7 (Em)
C7 (A7)
F (D)
su - jet de ma joie, al - le - lu - ia!
voice to tell my joy. Al - le - lu - ia!

2 *Dieu, l'Éternel est roi, il règne à jamais.*
Pour le jugement, il dresse son trône:
il jugera la terre,
Dieu, l'Éternel est roi, il règne à jamais.
Le monde verra la force de son bras,
alleluia!

3 *Dieu voit les opprimés, il est leur abri,*
leur refuge au temps des grandes détresses.
Son nom est leur salut.
Dieu voit les opprimés, il est leur abri,
il sauve les siens, car il est le Dieu Saint,
alleluia!

4 *Gloire au Père et au Fils et au Saint-Esprit*
au commencement, aujourd'hui, toujours
et aux siècles des siècles.
Gloire au Père et au Fils et au Saint-Esprit
d'une éternité à l'autre éternité,
alleluia!

2 No limits to the power of his mighty hand!
We'll come to his throne, his justice to be known –
for all to understand.
No limits to the power of his mighty hand –
creation will see how just and true is he.
Alleluia!

3 With justice he is kind – he knows we are weak.
His children in pain will rise up again –
he loves to help the meek.
With justice he is kind – he knows we are weak;
the God we adore is faithful to the poor.
Alleluia!

4 Sing out your praise to God the Three-in-One –
we'll sing of the Lord, the Spirit, the Word,
till earthly time is done.
Sing out your praise to God the Three-in-One –
we'll meet and adore when time shall be no more.
Alleluia!

45 JESU TAWA PANO

Jesus, we are here

ZIMBABWE

Words and music: Patrick Matsikenyiri

With expression ♩ = 100
E
B7
F♯m/B
Je - su ta - wa pa - no; Je - su
Je - sus, we are here; Je - sus,
E
Emaj7
E
E7
A
ta - wa pa - no; Je - su ta - wa pa - no;
we are here; Je - sus, we are here;
A9
A6
E/B
B9
B7
E
(except last time)
Mam - bo Je - su.
ta - wa pa - no mu zi - ta re - nyu.
we are here for you.

A gathering song, originally from Shona, and composed by Patrick Matsikenyiri, a primary school headmaster and a leading composer of African Church music. The harmonic clash in bar five is deliberate. Patrick said to John Bell of the Iona Community, 'If you knew the history of our country, you would know that we have had so many clashes that a little difficulty in the harmony will cause us no problem.' Other verses may be added e.g. We are here *with* you, . . . *in* you.

46 JESU, JESU, FILL US WITH YOUR LOVE

GHANA

Words: Tom Colvin
Music: Ghanaian melody
arranged Geoff Weaver

With a gentle lilt ♩. = 63

Chorus PARTS
Capo 1(E) F (E)
Am (G#m) Gm (F#m)
Je - su, Je - su, fill us with your love; show
Je - su, Je - su
Gm/C F (E) Dm7 (C#m) Gm (F#m) C7 (B7) F (E)
Fine
us how to serve the neigh-bors we have from you.
UNISON
Dm7 (C#m7) Gm (F#m) C7 (B7)
1 Kneels at the feet of his friends, si - lent-ly wash - es their
2 Neigh-bors are rich folk and poor; neigh-bors are black, brown and
3 These are the ones we should serve, these are the ones we should
4 Lov - ing puts us on our knees, serv - ing as though we were

One of the many hymns from Ghana originally collected by Tom Colvin. This 'song of service' has been included in many modern hymn books in recent years.
Suggested drum pattern: 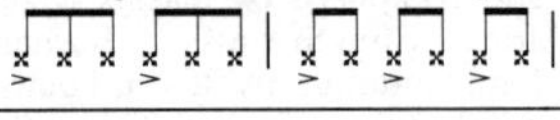

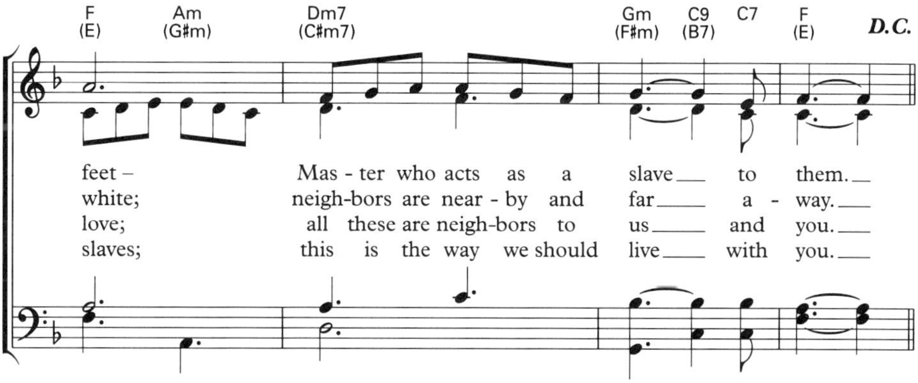
F (E) Am (G#m) Dm7 (C#m7) Gm (F#m) C9 (B7) C7 F (E)
D.C.
feet – Mas - ter who acts as a slave to them.
white; neigh-bors are near - by and far a - way.
love; all these are neigh-bors to us and you.
slaves; this is the way we should live with you.

Jesu, Jesu, fill us with your love;
show us how to serve the neighbors we have from you.

1 Kneels at the feet of his friends,
silently washes their feet –
Master who acts as a slave to them.
Jesu, Jesu . . .

2 Neighbors are rich folk and poor;
neighbors are black, brown and white;
neighbors are nearby and far away.
Jesu, Jesu . . .

3 These are the ones we should serve,
these are the ones we should love;
all these are neighbors to us and you.
Jesu, Jesu . . .

4 Loving puts us on our knees,
serving as though we were slaves;
this is the way we should live with you.
Jesu, Jesu . . .

47 JESUS THE LORD SAID

INDIA

Words: anonymous
translated Dermott Monahan
Music: Urdu melody
arranged Geoff Weaver

Steadily ♩ = 88
C G/B C C/E G/B C Dm/F
1 Je - sus the Lord said: 'I am the Bread, the Bread of___ Life for the
2 Je - sus the Lord said: 'I am the Door, the Way and the Door for the
3 Je - sus the Lord said: 'I am the Light, the one true_ Light of the
C/G G C Dm7 C/E F6 F G
world am I. The Bread of___ Life for the world am I, the
poor am I. The Way and the Door for the poor am I, the
world am I. The one true_ Light of the world am I, the
Am Em G/D D7 G C G/B
Bread of___ Life for the world am I.' Je - sus the Lord said:
Way and the Door for the poor am I.' Je - sus the Lord said:
one true_ Light of the world am I.' Je - sus the Lord said:

One of the most widely travelled of Indian hymns, this haunting melody is Urdu in origin. It makes an ideal vehicle through which to teach many of Jesus' sayings about himself, and may be expanded ad lib.

1 Jesus the Lord said: 'I am the Bread,
the Bread of Life for the world am I.
The Bread of Life for the world am I,
the Bread of Life for the world am I.'
Jesus the Lord said: 'I am the Bread,
the Bread of Life for the world am I.'

2 Jesus the Lord said: 'I am the Door,
the Way and the Door for the poor am I . . .'

3 Jesus the Lord said: 'I am the Light,
the one true Light of the world am I . . .'

4 Jesus the Lord said: 'I am the Shepherd,
the one Good Shepherd of the sheep am I . . .'

5 Jesus the Lord said: 'I am the Life,
the Resurrection and the Life am I . . .'

48 JESUS, JESUS, HOW I ADORE YOU

Jai, Jai, Yisu

INDIA

Words: after C. D. Rockley
and in this version Word & Music
Music: Hindustani melody
arranged Geoff Weaver

♩ = 108

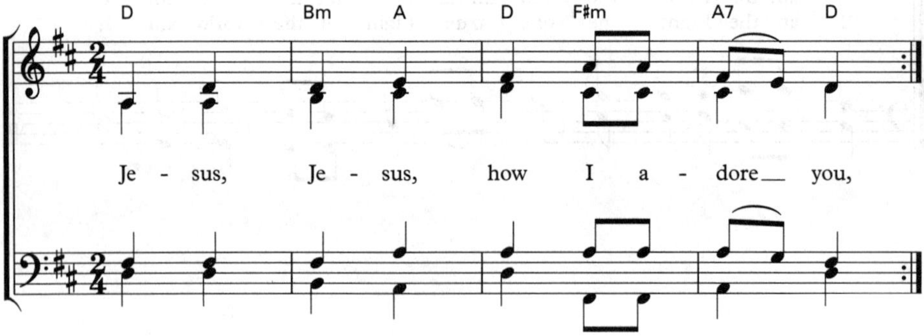
D Bm A D F#m A7 D
Je - sus, Je - sus, how I a - dore_ you,

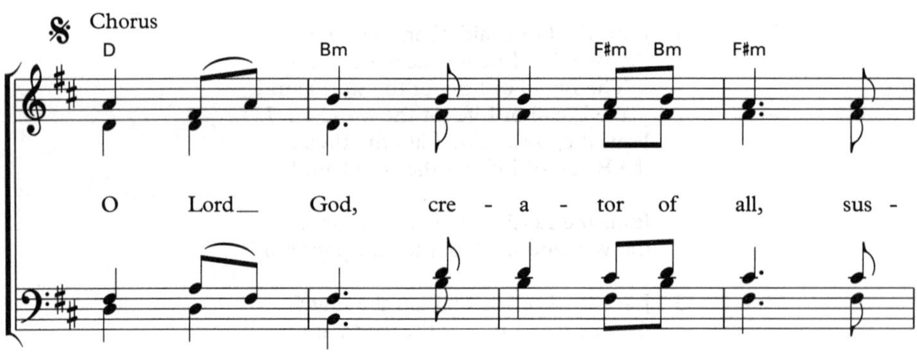
Chorus
D Bm F#m Bm F#m
O Lord_ God, cre - a - tor of all, sus -

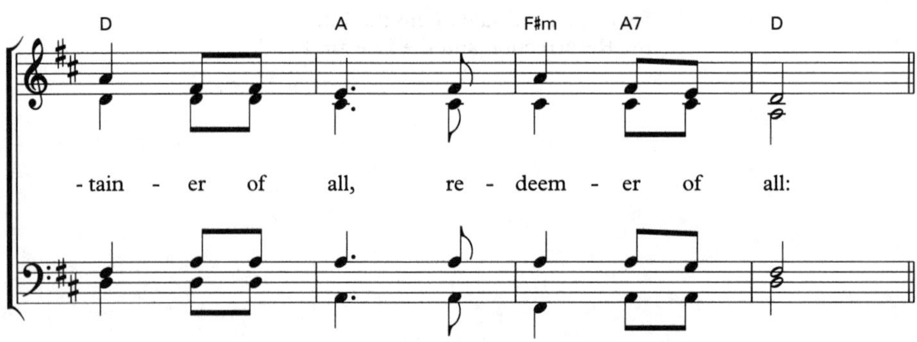
D A F#m A7 D
-tain - er of all, re - deem - er of all:

An earthy rhythmical refrain which is based on an Hindustani folk melody, and has something of the character of a folk dance. The verse should be more delicate in style.

Fine
D Bm A D F#m A7 D
Je - sus, Je - sus, how I a - dore you!
SOLO
D F#m Bm D/F#
1 Leav - ing your glo - ry, with love your great de - sign,
2 When I come to you in my pain
3 Al - le - lu - ia; glo - ry, glo - ry!
G D/F# Em Bm G A
giv - ing your life, and so re - deem - ing mine;
you give me your peace once a - gain;
Ev - ery - bo - dy, tell the sto - ry.
1st time SOLO
2nd time ALL (HARMONY)
D.S. al Fine
D Bm G Em Bm G F#m Bm
O Lord Je - sus, come; O Joy - giv - er come;
Re - liev - ing my load, guid - ing my road;
Come one, come all, come heed God's call;

49 JESUS CHRIST OUR LIVING LORD

HUNGARY

Words: after E. Turmezei
translated by E. Abraham and John L. Bell
Music: Szokolay Sandor
arranged Geoff Weaver

Steadily ♩ = 76
1 Je - sus Christ, our liv - ing Lord, we be - lieve you
2 In the humbl - est things we do we'll ac - count our -
3 Food e - nough that all may feed, grace e - nough for
4 Lord in all we do to - day let our lives pre -
keep your word: what - ev - er may be - fall us,
- selves to you; mak - ing your love our mea - sure,
each one's need - even as we praise you, sing - ing
- pare your way; may peace and love be - friend us
stretch or stall us, we'll trust your voice to call us.
truth and trea - sure, your will our joy and plea - sure.
you come bring - ing gifts at the day's be - gin - ning.
and de - fend us wher - ev - er you may send us.

Folk-song like in character, this hymn was published in a new hymnbook produced in 1981 by the Hungarian Ecumenical Council of Churches.

50 KAY YAHWEH AKO

I'll follow my Lord

PHILIPPINES

Words: from the Tagalog
in this version Word & Music
Music: unknown
arranged Geoff Weaver

Relaxed, easy flow ♩ = 88

Bm F#m G D
Kay Yah - weh a - ko, kay Yah - weh a - ko Kay
I'll fol - low my Lord, I'll fol - low my Lord, I'll
F#7/C# Bm Em6/G F# F#7
Yah - weh a - ko ma - na - na - na - gan Kay
fol - low my Lord – to Je - sus I cling; I'll
Bm F#m G D
Yah - weh a - ko, kay Yah - weh a - ko, Kay
fol - low my Lord, I'll fol - low my Lord, I'll
F#7/C# Bm F#7 Bm
Yah - weh a - ko ma - na - na - gan.
fol - low my Lord – my love I will bring!

The arranger heard this beautiful song sung by Filipino Christians who had recently suffered devastation from earthquake, volcanic eruption and typhoon. In that context, to sing, 'to Jesus I cling', has tremendous power and relevance. Its folk-song character is well served by a guitar accompaniment.

51 KATA KU NA NI MO SHU O KOBA MI NU

Here I am, the one

JAPAN

Words: Yukiko Ishiyama
translated Yasuhiko Yokosaka
paraphrased James Minchin
Music: Akira Tanaka
arranged Geoff Weaver

Flowing 𝅗𝅥 = 69

Capo 3(Bm)

N.C.
1 Ka - ta ku na ni mo shu o ko - ba mi nu, i -
2 O ro ka na ru ma - yo - i na ri shi ka, hi -
1 Here I am, the one who turned from Yah-weh, my God: how
2 Dark-ness swal-lowed hope as I con - ti - nued in sin: how
Dm (Bm) Am/C (F#m) B♭ (G) F (D) Dm (Bm) Am (F#m)
- to ke na ki wa re. I - ma wa
- to to - ki no wa re. I - ma wa
stub - born my re - sis - tance! What shall I
fright - en - ing the dark - ness! Far from my
Gm (Em) Am (F#m) Gm/B (Em) Dm/A (Bm) Gm7 (Em7) Gm/E A (F#) N.C.
shú no mi - ko - ko - ro o, mo - to - me tsu -
shú no mi - ko - ko - ro o, a - o - gi tsu -
do to find for - give - ness now? I will pray and
home, I was be - wil - dered, lost. Now I go forth

There is an austere joy in this song of repentance and new life, perhaps reflecting the often turbulent history of the small Christian community in Japan.

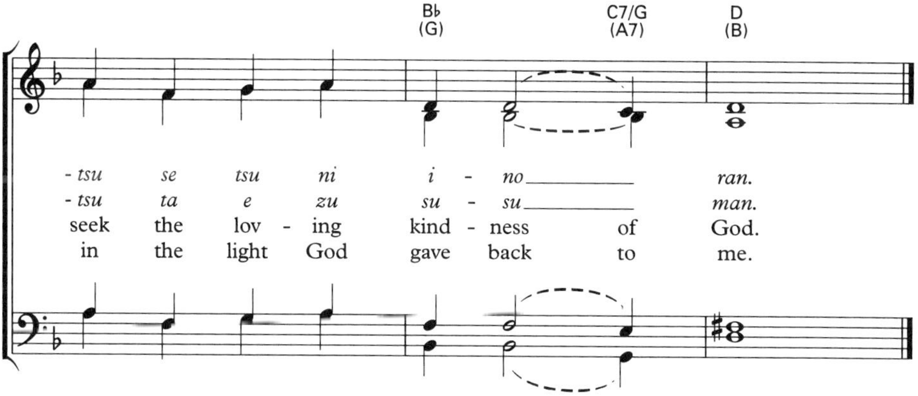
B♭ (G)
C7/G (A7)
D (B)
-tsu se tsu ni i - no ran.
-tsu ta e zu su - su man.
seek the lov - ing kind - ness of God.
in the light God gave back to me.

1 *Kata ku na ni mo shu o koba mi nu,*
ito ke na ki wa re.
Ima wa shú no mikokoro o,
motome tsutsu se tsu ni ino ran.

2 *O ro ka na ru mayoi na ri shi ka,*
hito toki no wa re.
Ima wa shú no mikokoro o,
aogi tsutsu ta e zu susu man.

3 *No ni yama ni hikari ahure te,*
suku wa re shi wa re.
Ima wa shú no mimegumi o,
Taka raka ni tatae uta wan.

1 Here I am, the one who turned from Yahweh, my God:
how stubborn my resistance!
What shall I do to find forgiveness now?
I will pray and seek the loving kindness of God.

2 Darkness swallowed hope as I continued in sin:
how frightening the darkness!
Far from my home, I was bewildered, lost.
Now I go forth in the light God gave back to me.

3 All around, the landscape shines with new light and life,
the fields and mountains glisten!
Jesus' salvation fills the world with joy.
I will praise and sing God's goodness while I have breath.

52 KATIKA SAFARI

On the journey to heaven

KENYA

Words and music: unknown
English: Word & Music
arranged Geoff Weaver

March-like ♩ = 112

G C G D G C G
1 Ka - ti - ka sa - fa - ri ya kwen - da m(bin)-gu - ni
2 U - ki - wa u - si - ku u - ki - wa mch - an - a
3 U - ki - fi - ka ku - le, u - ta - pum zi - ka
1 On the jour - ney to hea - ven we'll walk with the Lord,
2 On the jour - ney to hea - ven we'll live in the light,
3 On the jour - ney to hea - ven he'll give us his rest,
Tem - be - a na Bwa - na Ye - su, Ka - ti - ka sa - fa - ri ya kwen - da m(bin)-gu - ni
Tem - be - a na Bwa - na Ye - su, U - ki - wa u - si - ku u - ki - wa mch - an - a
Tem - be - a na Bwa - na Ye - su, U - ki - fi - ka ku - le, u - ta - pum zi - ka
he will walk with us on our way; when we walk with the Lord he will lead by his word –
he will shine light up - on our way; when we live in the light we shall not fear the night –
he will give rest up - on our way; when he gives us his rest, we'll know his way is best –

The Christian life is often portrayed as a journey, following the Way, and this East African song has a typical exuberance and rhythmic vitality, depicting the march of the pilgrims. Add descants and drums ad lib.

G/D D7 G
Tem - be-a na Bwa-na Ye - su. Tem - be-a na - e,
Tem - be-a na Bwa-na Ye - su. Tem - be-a na - e,
Tem - be-a na Bwa-na Ye - su. Tem - be-a na - e,
Je - sus is with us ev - ery day. Je - sus is with us,
Je - sus is with us, come what may. Je - sus is with us,
Je - sus is with us when we pray. Je - sus is with us,
C G
Tem - be - a na - e, Tem - be - a na Bwa-na Ye -
Tem - be - a na - e, Tem - be - a na Bwa-na Ye -
Tem - be - a na - e, Tem - be - a na Bwa-na Ye -
Je - sus is with us, Je - sus is with us ev - ery
Je - sus is with us, Je - sus is with us ev - ery
Je - sus is with us, Je - sus is with us when we
D7 G C G
- su. Ka - ti - ka sa fa ri ya kwen - da m(bin)-gu - ni
- su. U - ki - wa u - si - ku u - ki - wa mch - an - a
- su. U - ki - fi - ka ku-le, u - ta - pum zi - ka
day. On the jour - ney to hea - ven we'll walk with the Lord,
day. On the jour - ney to hea - ven we'll live in the light,
pray. On the jour - ney to hea - ven he'll give us his rest,
G/D D7 G
Tem - be - a na Bwa - na Ye - su.
Tem - be - a na Bwa - na Ye - su.
Tem - be - a na Bwa - na Ye - su.
he will walk with us on our way.
he will shine light up - on our way.
he will give rest up - on our way.

53 KOSKETA MINUA, HENKI

Touch me, God's Spirit

FINLAND

Words: Anna-Maija Raittila
English: Matti Kilpio
Music: Ilkka Kuusisto
arranged Geoff Weaver

Flowing ♩ = 144

Capo 3(G)
B♭ (G) Dm (Bm) Gm (Em) Cm (Am)
1 Kos - ke - ta mi - nu - a, Hen - ki! Kos - ke - ta,
2 Kos - ke - ta, Ju - ma - lan Hen - ki, sy - väl - le
1 Touch me, God's Spi - rit e - ter - nal, touch me, res -
2 Touch me, God's Spi - rit, and soothe me deep in my
Dm7 (Bm7) E♭ (C) G7/D (E7) Cm7 (Am7) F9 (D7)
kirk - ka - us! An - na e - lä -
sy - däme - en. Sin - ne pa - ina
- plen - dent Light; give my life new
rest - less soul; give me trust in
B♭maj7 (G) G7sus (E) G7 Cm7 (Am7) F (D7) F7 B♭ (G)
- mäl - le suun - ta ja tar - koi - tus.
hil - jaa luot - ta - mus Je - esuk - seen.
mean - ing, show me the true and right.
Je - sus, heal me and make me whole.

A gentle song of invitation to the Holy Spirit from the Christian community in Finland.

1 *Kosketa minua, Henki!*
Kosketa, kirkkaus!
Anna elämälle
suunta ja tarkoitus.

2 *Kosketa, Jumalan Henki,*
syvälle sydämeen.
Sinne paina hiljaa
luottamus Jeesukseen.

3 *Rohkaise minua, Henki,*
murenna pelkoni.
Tässä maailmassa
osoita paikkani.

4 *Valaise, Jumalan Henki,*
silmäni aukaise,
että voisin olla
ystävä toisille.

5 *Kosketa minua, Henki!*
Herätä kiittämään,
sinun lähelläsi
armosta elämään.

1 Touch me, God's Spirit eternal,
touch me, resplendent Light;
give my life new meaning,
show me the true and right.

2 Touch me, God's Spirit, and soothe me
deep in my restless soul;
give me trust in Jesus,
heal me and make me whole.

3 Spirit of God, give me courage,
banish my doubts and fears;
show me my vocation
through all my days and years.

4 Spirit of God, brightly shining,
open my eyes to see
those who need my friendship –
join us in unity.

5 Touch me, God's Spirit eternal,
teach me to thank and praise;
by your grace be near me,
guide me in all my ways.

54 KUNIN MO ANG AKING PUSO

Let me tell you how I need you

PHILIPPINES

Words and music: Teresita Valeriano
English: Word & Music
music arranged Geoff Weaver

With intensity ♩ = 72

Capo 1(Am)
B♭m (Am)
E♭m (Dm)
1 Ku - nin Mo ang a - king pu - so;
2 Ku - nin Mo ang a - king bu - hay;
1 Let me tell you how I need you;
2 In your mer - cy, Lord, for - give me,
F7 (E7)
B♭m (Am)
ku - sang i - bi - ni - bi - gay i - to. He -
sa 'Yo a - king i - na - a - lay. He -
take my love, I give it to___ you: for
by your grace come, cleanse, re - new___ me: for
G♭ (F)
E♭m6 (Dm)
D♭/F (C)
Fm (Em)
- sus ang 'Yong pag - ma - ma-hal ang ma -
- sus sa 'Yong ka - la - ka - san ay na -
you have died to___ bring me life – O Lord
you a - lone can___ change my life – O Lord

A rich and passionate 'prayer in song', composed by a former student at the Asian School for Music, Worship and the Arts in Manila, and firmly rooted in her vibrant Filipino culture. Allow the alternation between four and three beats in a bar to flow naturally.

E♭m7 (Dm7)
Cm9 (Bm7)
F7 (E7)
-na - na - han sa pu - song pa - gal.
-is ki - tang ma - pag - ling - ku - ran.
Je - sus Christ, you're my heart's de - sire!
Je - sus Christ, you're the liv - ing fire.
B♭m (Am)
E♭m (Dm)
F7 (E7)
Da - hil I - kaw ang bu - hay at ang ka - to - to-
Je - sus, I want to know you, Je - sus, I want to
B♭m (Am)
E♭m7 (Dm7)
- ha - nan, a - king i - si - nu -
serve you; Je - sus, I want to
D♭/F (C)
F7 (E7)
B♭m (Am)
- su - ko bu - hay na mu - la sa - 'Yo.
love you – love you more, to love you more.

55 KYRIE ELEISON

Lord, have mercy

Russia

Kyrie

Words: traditional
Music: Russian Orthodox

Slowly ♩ = 60

Ky - ri - e e - lei - son. Ky - ri - e e - lei - son.
Lord, ___ have mer - cy. Lord, ___ have mer - cy.
Ky - ri - e e - lei - son.
Lord, ___ have mer - cy.

Kyrie eleison.
Kyrie eleison.
Kyrie eleison.

Lord, have mercy.
Lord, have mercy.
Lord, have mercy.

Originally from the Russian Orthodox Church, this simple chant is ideal for encouraging a congregation to sing in harmony. It may be used repeatedly as a focus for meditation.

56 KYRIE ELEISON

Lord, have mercy

GHANA

Words: traditional
Music: Dinah Reindorf
arranged Geoff Weaver

Expressively ♩ = 76
Capo 3(Am)
Cm (Am) F7/C (D7) Gaug/C (E) Cm (Am)
Ky - ri - e e - le - i - son. Ky - ri - e e -
Lord, have mer - cy. Lord, have
F9 (D) Gaug (E) G7 Cm (Am) Cm7 (Am7) F7 (D7) D7(add F) (B7)
-le - i - son. Ky - ri - e e - le - i son.
mer - cy. Lord, have mer - cy.
Bdim (G♯dim) Cm/G (Am) Fm(♭9) (Dm) Cm (Am)
Ky - ri - e e - lei son.
Lord, have mer - cy on us.

It is not too fanciful to hear in this expressive Kyrie, with echoes of the blues in its final phrase, so much of the pain and suffering of Ghana's colonial past with its slave trade and enforced break-up of families. Dinah Reindorf, one of Ghana's leading musicians, composed this in response to a Passion Walk, walking in Christ's footsteps to the cross.

57 LA VENIDA DE CRISTO

When the stars in their flight

CHILE

Dance-like 𝅗𝅥. = 66

Words: Santiago Stevenson
English: From Mark 13, Michael Perry
Music: Chilean melody
arranged Geoff Weaver

Capo 1(Bm)
TWO PARTS
Cm (Bm)
G7 (F♯)
1 La ve - ni - da de Cris - to se a - ce - rca. Pron - to
2 Si que - re - mos que Cris - to nos lle - ve a los
1 When the stars in their flight fall from the hea - vens, and the
2 Be on guard! Be pre-pared for Je - sus' com - ing; for we
Cm (Bm)
vie - ne su i - gle - sia a bus - car. No dur -
cie - los con él a mo - rar. No se -
world has sur - ren - dered to night, and the
don't know the day or the hour, but we'll
G7 (F♯7)
Cm (Bm)
A♭7 (G7)
- ma - mos, es - te - mos a - ler - tos; ¡Vi - gi -
- a - mos ja - más ne - gli - gen - tes; ¡Tra - ba -
pil - lars of earth have been sha - ken, and the
hear of the wars of the na - tions, when the
Cm/G (Bm)
G (F♯)
Cm (Bm)
- lad, vi - gi - lad, vi - gi - lad!
- jad, tra - ba - jad, tra - ba - jad!
sun and the moon lose their light:
kings of the earth lose their power.
Pron - to
Then we'll

There has been astonishing growth in the Protestant churches in Latin America in recent years. New Christians are encouraged to sing songs which grow from their own culture, and this lively dance song is a good example of such 'enculturation'. Add percussion instruments and guitars as you wish.

B♭ (A)
E♭ (D)
vie - ne Je - sús y nos lle - va a la her -
see the Lord come in his glo - ry, in the
B♭7 (A7)
E♭ (D)
G/B (F♯)
G
- mo - sa man-sión ce - les - tial. Pron-to vie - ne Je - sús a la
clouds he'll des-cend from his throne; he will send all his an - gels be-
Cm (Bm)
A♭ (G)
UNISON
Cm/G (Bm)
G7 (F♯7)
Cm (Bm)
tie - rra; nos i - re - mos con él a mo - rar.
- fore him, and with joy they will ga - ther his own.

3 *Arreglemos, estemos a cuentas*
con Jesús, el Cordero de Dios.
Del que ofende tengamos clemencia;
¡Perdonad, perdonad, perdonad!
Pronto viene . . .

4 *Perdonando, Jesús nos perdona,*
y nos lleva con él a reinar.
Ganaremos también la corona;
¡Vigilad, trabajad, perdonad!
Pronto viene . . .

3 We can trust in the presence of the Spirit,
he will teach us what we are to say;
and we need not be fearful or anxious,
for his grace will provide in that day.
Then we'll see the Lord . . .

4 When the leaves of the fig tree are emerging,
then we see that the summer is near,
even so, as these things start to happen
then you know that the Son will appear.
Then we'll see the Lord . . .

58 LAUDATE DOMINUM

Sing praise and bless the Lord

FRANCE

Words: from Psalm 117
Music: Jacques Berthier
Taizé Community

Joyfully ♩ = 116

OSTINATO – MIXED VOICES

EQUAL VOICES

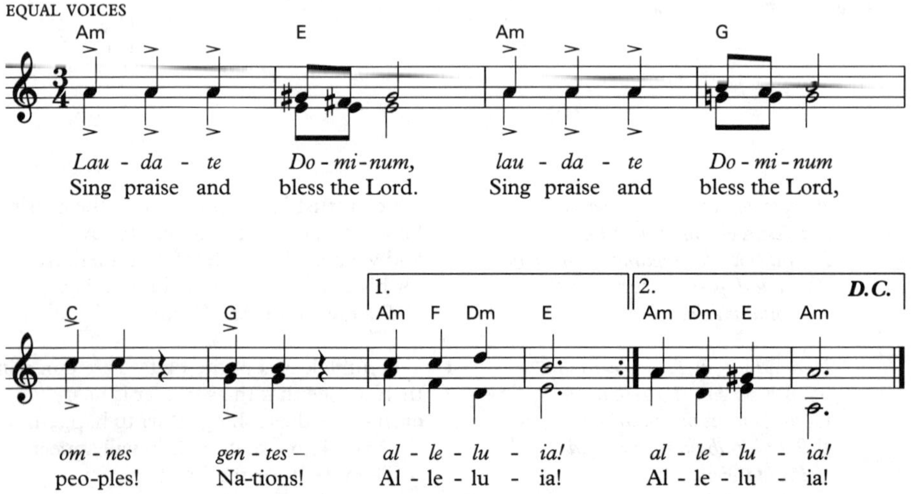

A powerful Taizé chant suitable for times of praise and celebration.

SOLO VERSES (sung above OSTINATO)

Am E Am G
1 Praise__ the Lord, all you na - tions, praise God,
C G Am F Dm E
all you__ peo - ples – Al - le - lu - ia.
Am E Am G
Strong is God's love and mer - cy, God is
C G Am Dm E Am
faith - ful for ev - er – Al - le - lu - ia! 2 Al - le -
Am E Am G
- lu - ia, al - le - lu - ia let
C G Am F Dm E
ev - ery - thing liv - ing give praise to the Lord! Al - le -
Am E Am G
- lu - ia, al - le - lu - ia – let
C G Am Dm E Am
ev - ery - thing liv - ing give praise to the Lord!

59 LET US GREET ONE ANOTHER

JAMAICA

Words: Jamaican greeting song
Music: unknown
arranged David Peacock

Rhythmically ♩ = 120
E E/G# A B E E/G#
Let us greet one an-oth-er in Je - sus' name, let us greet some - bo-dy in
A B E E/G# A B E
Je - sus' name, let us tell them that we love them in Je - sus' name; tell them
E/G# A B7 E A/E E E/G#
we can work to-geth-er in Je - sus' name. Ev-ery-bo-dy smile — Je-sus
A B7 E A/E E E/G# A B7 E
loves you! Ev-ery-bo-dy smile — Je - sus loves you!

It is difficult to feel excluded when worshipping in the Caribbean. This song would be ideal for the exchange of greetings or the Peace.

60 LOE DE ÍSÁ

Jesus knows the inmost heart

PAKISTAN

Words: from the Pushto, Alison Blenkinsop
Music: unknown
arranged Geoff Weaver

Flowing ♩. = 60

Chorus HARMONY

repeat first time only

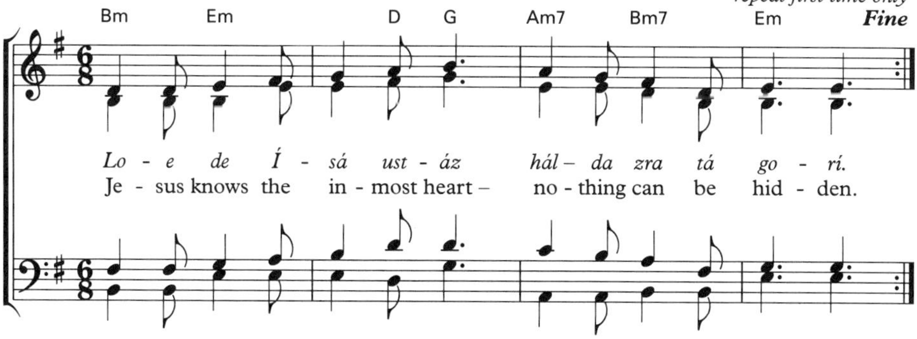

Bm Em D G Am7 Bm7 Em
Fine
Lo - e de Í - sá ust - áz hál – da zra tá go - rí.
Je - sus knows the in - most heart – no - thing can be hid - den.

Verse UNISON

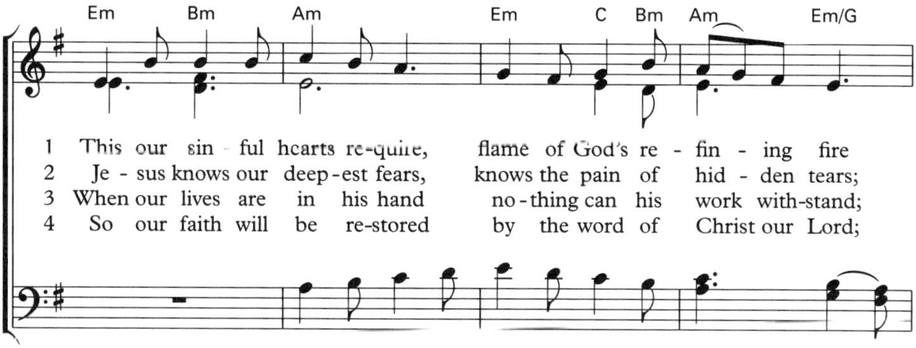

Em Bm Am Em C Bm Am Em/G
1 This our sin - ful hearts re-quire, flame of God's re - fin - ing fire
2 Je - sus knows our deep-est fears, knows the pain of hid - den tears;
3 When our lives are in his hand no-thing can his work with-stand;
4 So our faith will be re-stored by the word of Christ our Lord;

D.C.

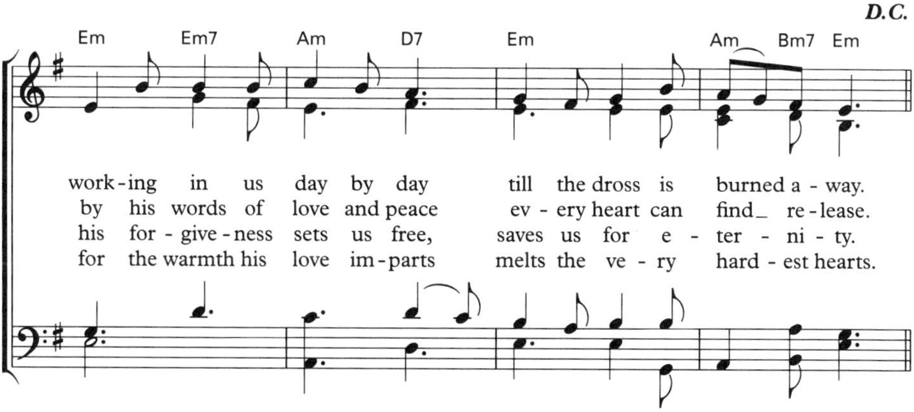

Em Em7 Am D7 Em Am Bm7 Em
work-ing in us day by day till the dross is burned a - way.
by his words of love and peace ev - ery heart can find_ re-lease.
his for - give-ness sets us free, saves us for e - ter - ni - ty.
for the warmth his love im-parts melts the ve - ry hard - est hearts.

One of a number of songs from the Pushto-speaking Christians of Pakistan which have been collected by Alison Blenkinsop (formerly Fookes), who served as a missionary there. Both melody and text have a simplicity and directness which is very appealing.

61 LOOK AND LEARN

KOREA

Words: from Matthew 6: 23–34
John L. Bell
Music: Nah Young-Soo
arranged Geoff Weaver

Flowing ♩. = 56

G
C6/G
G
D
1 Look and learn from the birds of the air, fly - ing high a-bove
2 Look and learn from the flowers of the field, bring - ing beau - ty and
3 What God wants_ should be___ our will; where God calls_ should
C/G
D7/G
G
C/G
G
C
G
wor - ry and fear; nei - ther sow - ing nor har - vest-ing seed,
col - or to life; nei - ther sew - ing nor tail - or-ing cloth,
be___ our goal. When we seek___ the King - dom first,
D
C/G
D7
G
yet they're gi - ven what - ev - er they need. If the God of
yet they're dressed in the fin - est at - tire. If the God of
all we've lost___ is ours___ a - gain. Let's be done with

On hearing this haunting pentatonic melody, many people are surprised to learn of its Korean origin. This should have an easy flow, not moving too slowly.

Em Bm Am D9 D7
earth and heaven cares for birds as much__ as this,
earth and heaven cares for flowers as much__ as this,
anx - ious thoughts, set a - side to - mor - row's cares,
G C/G G C G D C/G D7 G
won't he care much more for you, if you put your trust_ in him?
won't he care much more for you if you put_ your trust_ in him?
live each day_ that God pro-vides put - ting all__ our trust_ in him.

1 Look and learn from the birds of the air,
flying high above worry and fear;
neither sowing nor harvesting seed,
yet they're given whatever they need.
If the God of earth and heaven
cares for birds as much as this,
won't he care much more for you,
if you put your trust in him?

2 Look and learn from the flowers of the field,
bringing beauty and color to life;
neither sewing nor tailoring cloth,
yet they're dressed in the finest attire.
If the God of earth and heaven
cares for flowers as much as this,
won't he care much more for you
if you put your trust in him?

3 What God wants should be our will;
where God calls should be our goal.
When we seek the Kingdom first,
all we've lost is ours again.
Let's be done with anxious thoughts,
set aside tomorrow's cares,
live each day that God provides
putting all our trust in him.

62 LORD, FORGIVE ME

CHINA

Words: Ellsworth Candlee
Music: Confucian Chant
arranged Geoff Weaver

♩ = 92
1 Lord, for - give___ me. Christ, have mer - cy!
2 Lord, for - give___ me. Christ, have mer - cy!
ORGAN PEDAL
I con - fess to you all my sin and shame.
Now to turn from sin, Lord, grant heaven - ly grace.
Save me, Lord, I cry. In your cross I trust,
Raised up and re-newed, may I fol - low you,

In the early 20th century, it was often said in China 'One Christian more means one Chinese less.' The use of an ancient Confucian chant in worship is one way in which Chinese Christians are able to root their faith in their Chinese culture and traditions.

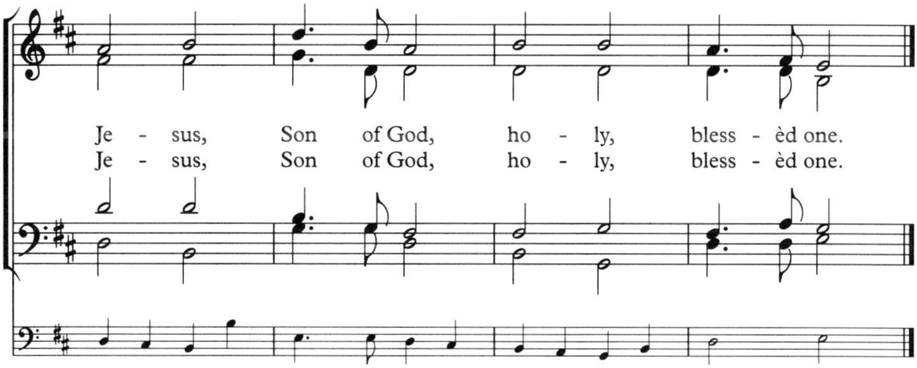
Je - sus, Son of God, ho - ly, bless - èd one.
Je - sus, Son of God, ho - ly, bless - èd one.

1 Lord, forgive me. Christ, have mercy!
I confess to you all my sin and shame.
Save me, Lord, I cry.
In your cross I trust,
Jesus, Son of God, holy, blessèd one.

2 Lord, forgive me. Christ, have mercy!
Now to turn from sin, Lord,
grant heavenly grace.
Raised up and renewed,
may I follow you,
Jesus, Son of God, holy, blessèd one.

63 MAJESTET, KONGE I EVIGHET

Majesty, King of eternity

NORWAY

Words and music: Jan Honningdal
English: Word & Music
arranged David Peacock

Sensitively 𝅗𝅥 = 70

A
E E7/G#
Ma - jes - tet, Kon - ge i e - vig - het,
Ma - jes - ty, King of e - ter - ni - ty
A G/B A/C# D A/C#
Jord og hav og him - mel,
earth and sea and hea - ven,
G G/F# E E7 A
alt er skapt av deg. Ma - jes - tet,
all are your de - sign. Ma - jes - ty,
E E7/G# A G/B A/C#
Kon - ge i e - vig - het,
King of e - ter - ni - ty

A recent worship song from Norway which needs to be 'held-back' rather than rushed.

D
A/C#
du, en borg til frel - se, et
you're our strength and re - fuge,
Bm7
Esus
E
D/E
sik - kert skju - le - sted.
you're our hid - ing - place.
Vi vil opp -
We will a -
A
D
E
- høy - e deg,
Kong Je -
- dore you,
King Je -
C#m
D
E
D/F#
E7/G#
A
- sus.
Hvert et kne skal bøy - e seg for
- sus –
ev - ery knee shall bow be - fore your
G
E7
D/E
A
deg.
Vi vil opp - høy - e deg,
throne;
we will a - dore you,

D
E
C#m
Kong Je - sus.
King Je - sus –
D
A/C#
Bm7
A/B
Ing - en er som du, nei, in - gen
there is none like you, no, there is
Bm7/E
A
er som du.
none like you.

Majestet, Konge i evighet,
Jord og hav og himmel,
alt er skapt av deg.
Majestet, Konge i evighet,
du, en borg til frelse,
et sikkert skjulested.
Vi vil opphøye deg, Kong Jesus.
Hvert et kne skal bøye seg for deg.
Vi vil opphøye deg, Kong Jesus.
Ingen er som du,
nei, ingen er som du.

Majesty, King of eternity –
earth and sea and heaven,
all are your design.
Majesty, King of eternity –
you're our strength and refuge,
you're our hiding-place.
We will adore you, King Jesus –
every knee shall bow
before your throne;
we will adore you, King Jesus –
there is none like you,
no, there is none like you.

64 MAY THE PEACE OF GOD THE FATHER

Israel

Words: unknown
in this version Word & Music
Music: Israeli melody
arranged David Peacock

Flowing ♩ = 74

Dm F G
A May the peace of God the Fa - ther B and the grace of Christ, the
Am B♭
Son, A with the bless-ing of the Spi - rit –
F G Am F C
B God the ho - ly Three-in - One: A be up - on you
Dm Gm F C Dm
al-ways, and re-main B now and ev - er with you. A-men.

This haunting modal song of blessing is most effective when sung by two groups: the one responding to the other.

65 MAYENZIWE 'NTANDO YAKHO

Your will be done on earth

SOUTH AFRICA

Words: from the Lord's Prayer
Music: transcribed by John L. Bell

Not too fast ♩ = 96
E F#m/A
Ma - ye - nzi - we ___ 'nta -
Your will be done ___ on
Ma - ye - nzi - we ___ 'nta -
Your will be done ___ on
E/B B E F#/A
- ndo ya - kho. Ma - ye - nzi - we ___ 'nta -
earth, O Lord. Your will be done ___ on
- ndo ya - kho. Ma - ye - nzi - we ___ 'nta -
earth, O Lord. Your will be done ___ on
E/B B E F#m B7 E
- ndo ya - kho. Ma - ye - nzi - we ___ 'nta -
earth, O Lord. Your will ___ be done ___ on

A traditional song from South Africa, joyful and affirmative. This is best sung *a cappella*.

F♯m B7 E F♯m/A E/B B7
-ndo ya - kho. Ma - ye - nzi - we 'nta - ndo ya -
earth, O Lord. Your will be done on earth, O
E F♯m/A E/B B E
-kho. Ma - ye - nzi - we 'nta - ndo ya - kho.
Lord. Your will be done on earth, O Lord.

Mayenziwe 'ntando yakho.
Mayenziwe 'ntando yakho.
Mayenziwe 'ntando yakho.
Mayenziwe 'ntando yakho.
Mayenziwe 'ntando yakho.

Your will be done on earth, O Lord.
Your will be done on earth, O Lord.
Your will be done on earth, O Lord.
Your will be done on earth, O Lord.
Your will be done on earth, O Lord.

66 MWAMBA NI JESU
Who is the Rock

EAST AFRICA

Words and music: J. Nathan Corbitt

Confidently ♩ = 120

Capo 3(D)
F (D) Bb (G) C (A)
SOLO 1 *Mwam-ba, Mwam-ba?*
Who is the Rock?
(*only on repeat*)
ALL *Mwam-ba ni Je - su, Mwam-ba.*
The Rock is Je - sus, the Rock.
F (D) Bb (G) C (A) F (D)
D.C.
Mwam-ba, Mwam - ba?
Who is the Rock?
Mwam-ba ni Je - su, Mwam - ba.
The Rock is Je - sus, the Rock.

A song in the African call-response tradition. No books are required for the congregation and the song can be extended indefinitely as the soloist recalls the different attributes of Jesus the Rock.

1 SOLO *Mwamba, Mwamba?*
ALL *Mwamba ni Jesu, Mwamba.*
SOLO *Mwamba, Mwamba?*
ALL *Mwamba ni Jesu, Mwamba.*

2 SOLO *Abariki:*
ALL *Mwamba ni Jesu, Mwamba.*
SOLO *Abariki:*
ALL *Mwamba ni Jesu, Mwamba.*

3 SOLO *Anaponya:*
ALL *Mwamba ni Jesu, Mwamba.*
SOLO *Anaponya:*
ALL *Mwamba ni Jesu, Mwamba.*

4 SOLO *Analinda:*
ALL *Mwamba ni Jesu, Mwamba.*
SOLO *Analinda:*
ALL *Mwamba ni Jesu, Mwamba.*

5 SOLO *Aokoa:*
ALL *Mwamba ni Jesu, Mwamba.*
SOLO *Aokoa:*
ALL *Mwamba ni Jesu, Mwamba.*

6 SOLO *Mwamba . . .*

7 SOLO *Mwamba . . .*

1 SOLO Who is the Rock?
ALL The Rock is Jesus, the Rock.
SOLO Who is the Rock?
ALL The Rock is Jesus, the Rock.

2 SOLO He blesses us:
ALL the Rock is Jesus, the Rock.
SOLO He blesses us:
ALL the Rock is Jesus, the Rock.

3 SOLO He heals from sin:
ALL the Rock is Jesus, the Rock.
SOLO He heals from sin:
ALL the Rock is Jesus, the Rock.

4 SOLO The Rock protects:
ALL the Rock is Jesus, the Rock.
SOLO The Rock protects:
ALL the Rock is Jesus, the Rock.

5 SOLO He rescues us:
ALL the Rock is Jesus, the Rock.
SOLO He rescues us:
ALL the Rock is Jesus, the Rock.

6 SOLO Who is the Rock . . .

7 SOLO Who is the Rock . . .

67 MY SOUL WILL GLORIFY

INDONESIA

Words: from Luke 1
D. T. Niles
Music: Maluku popular song
arranged Geoff Weaver

Dance-like ♩. = 72

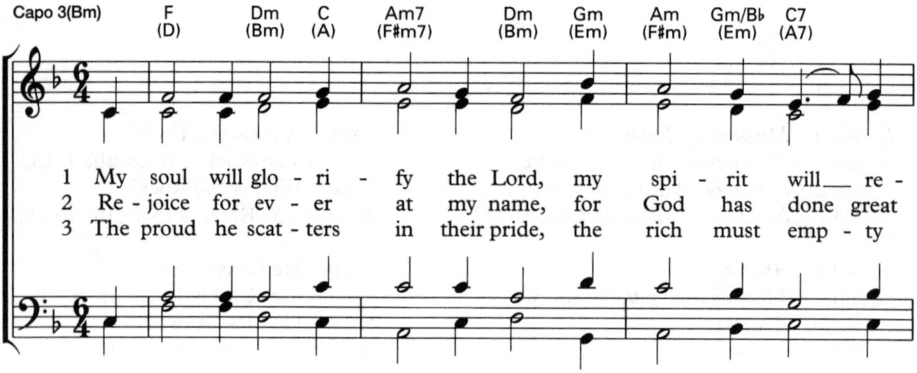

Capo 3(Bm)
F (D) Dm (Bm) C (A) Am7 (F#m7) Dm (Bm) Gm (Em) Am (F#m) Gm/B♭ (Em) C7 (A7)
1 My soul will glo - ri - fy the Lord, my spi - rit will re -
2 Re - joice for ev - er at my name, for God has done great
3 The proud he scat - ters in their pride, the rich must emp - ty

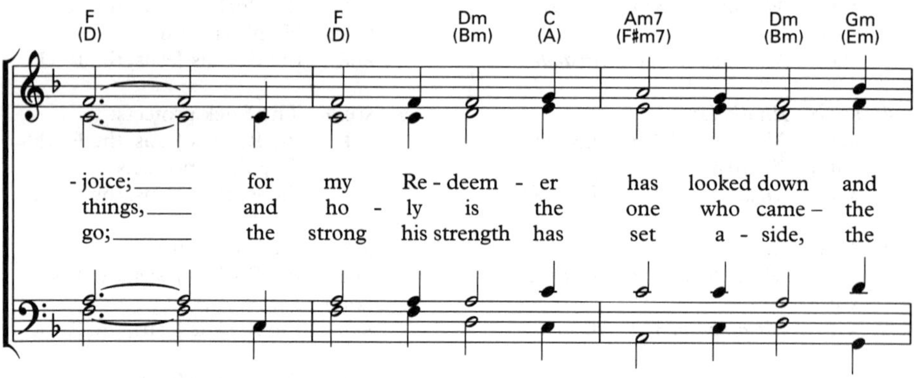

F (D) F (D) Dm (Bm) C (A) Am7 (F#m7) Dm (Bm) Gm (Em)
- joice; for my Re - deem - er has looked down and
things, and ho - ly is the one who came – the
go; the strong his strength has set a - side, the

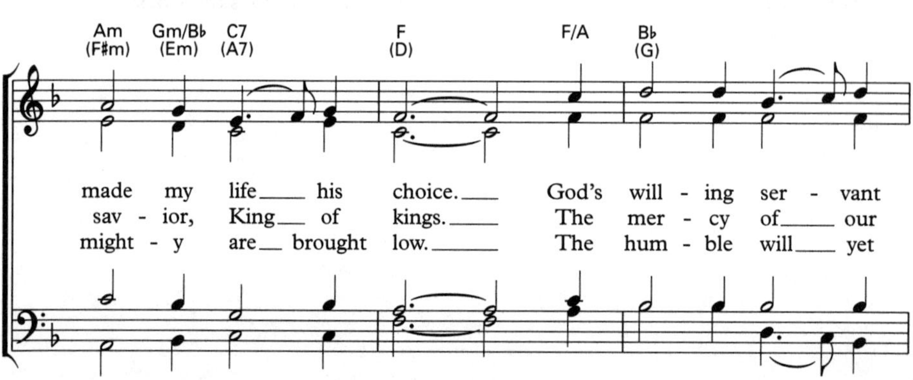

Am (F#m) Gm/B♭ (Em) C7 (A7) F (D) F/A B♭ (G)
made my life his choice. God's will - ing ser - vant
sav - ior, King of kings. The mer - cy of our
might - y are brought low. The hum - ble will yet

This captures beautifully the joy and the dance-like character of Mary's song. Ideally it should be sung unaccompanied.

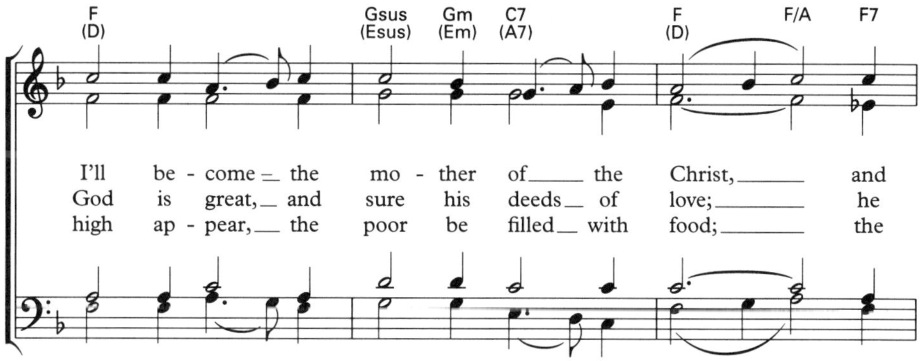
F (D) Gsus (Esus) Gm (Em) C7 (A7) F (D) F/A F7
I'll be - come the mo - ther of the Christ, and
God is great, and sure his deeds of love; he
high ap - pear, the poor be filled with food; the

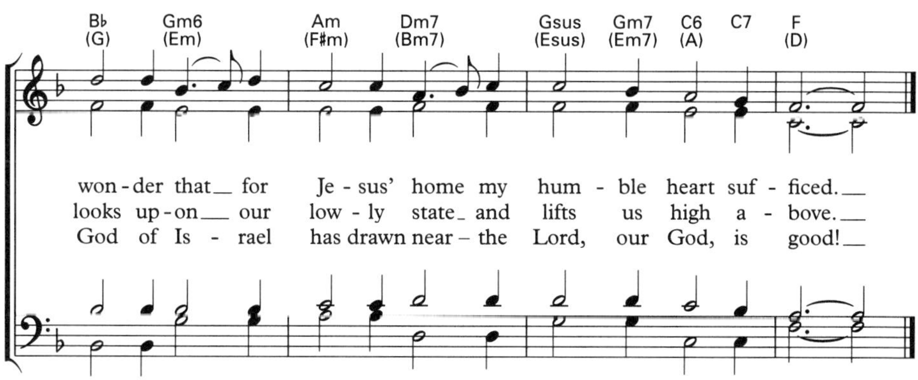
B♭ (G) Gm6 (Em) Am (F♯m) Dm7 (Bm7) Gsus (Esus) Gm7 (Em7) C6 (A) C7 F (D)
won - der that for Je - sus' home my hum - ble heart suf - ficed.
looks up - on our low - ly state and lifts us high a - bove.
God of Is - rael has drawn near – the Lord, our God, is good!

1 My soul will glorify the Lord,
my spirit will rejoice;
for my Redeemer has looked down
and made my life his choice.
God's willing servant I'll become –
the mother of the Christ,
and wonder that for Jesus' home
my humble heart sufficed.

2 Rejoice for ever at my name,
for God has done great things,
and holy is the one who came –
the savior, King of kings.
The mercy of our God is great,
and sure his deeds of love;
he looks upon our lowly state
and lifts us high above.

3 The proud he scatters in their pride,
the rich must empty go;
the strong his strength has set aside,
the mighty are brought low.
The humble will yet high appear,
the poor be filled with food;
the God of Israel has drawn near –
the Lord, our God, is good!

68 MOTO UMEWAKA LEO

God's fire

EAST AFRICA

Words and music: unknown
arranged Geoff Weaver

Lively ♩ = 108
G C G A D G C G G/D D7 G G/D D7 G
Mo - to u - me - wa - ka le - o, Mo - to ni ka - zi ya Ye - su, Mo - to u - me - wa - ka le - o; Tu - im - be hal - le - lu - jah mo - to u - me - wa - ka! Tu - im - be hal - le - lu - jah mo - to u - me - wa - ka!
God's fire is burn-ing in my soul, God's fire has come to make me whole, God's fire is sweep-ing through the earth; praise God, I've got God's fire and it's burn - ing in my soul! Praise God – yes, hal - le - lu - jah it's burn - ing in my soul!

A song which most probably came out of the East African revival.
It needs to be sung with rhythm, fire and commitment.

69

NA JIJOHO

Peace be with you

BENIN

Words: traditional
Music: unknown
arranged Geoff Weaver

Confidently ♩ = 104
D A7 D
SOLO ALL SOLO
Na Ji - jo - ho, ji - jo - ho ni tin. Na Ji - jo - ho,
Peace be with you, peace be__ with you. Peace be with you,
D A7 D D/F# G A
ALL
ji - jo - ho ni tin. Po__ ome - po - po, A -
peace be__ with you, with_ all of__ us, A -
ome-po-po, A -
all of us, A -
D D/F# G A D
- men. Po__ ome - po - po, A - men!
- men, with_ all of__ us, A - men!
- men ome - po - po, A - men!
- men all of us, A - men!

This song is very popular in Benin and is sung at thanksgiving and indeed on almost any occasion. It is simple enough to sing as greetings, or as the Peace is exchanged.

70 NGAIH CHIAT TAHNAK KA TON LID AH

When I am sad and sorrowful

MYANMAR

Words: unknown
in this version Word & Music
Music: unknown
arranged David Peacock

Lilting ♩ = 108

D G D
Ngaih chiat tah - nak ka ton lid ah, a ka hnum tu
When I am sad and sor - row - ful, Je - sus is there;
A
hawi tha bik cu Je - suh a si
he's my best friend, my Sa - vior.
D G D
dwat mi hna nih thlan mual ran - liam lid can zon - gah
When all my friends have gone a - way, in that sad day,
G D/A A7 D G D
bawi Je - suh nih a ka um - pi.
Je - sus my Lord is with me. More

The recent history of Myanmar (Burma) has been one of great oppression and suffering. The editor recently met a young man who dared not return home to his family and this song was sung to him by another radical young Christian who feared for the future of his country. Many families have lost loved ones and the words of this song must be truly heartfelt.

A A7 D/A A G D
Sui le ngun nak in sung deuh mi maw_ hawi tha
pre - cious than sil - ver or gold – he's my best friend;
G/D D Bm
ngaih chiat can ah lea thin hnem tu
when I am sad and sor - row - ful
Em7 A D
maw_ hawi tha ka nun nak al cheen
he's my best friend; he's al - ways pre - sent
G D
le zan in a ka um - pi. Hawi tha bik
day and night in my life. My best
G D/A A7 D G D
cu Je - suh a si.
friend is Je - sus.

71 NEEMA, NEEMA

Spirit of Jesus

EAST AFRICA

Words and music: unknown
arranged Geoff Weaver

= 96
G D7/G G C6 C G/D D7 G
Nee - ma, nee - ma, nee - ma i - me fu - nel-wa.
Spi - rit of Je - sus – Ho - ly Spi - rit, come to us.
Grace of the Fa - ther – Ho - ly Spi - rit, come to us.

Neema, neema,
neema ime funelwa.

Spirit of Jesus – Holy Spirit, come to us.
Grace of the Father – Holy Spirit, come to us.

A simple affirmation in song, ideal for a congregational response.

72 O LORD, HEAR MY PRAYER

FRANCE

Words: from Psalm 130
Music: Jacques Berthier

♩ = 54
Em Em7/D Am/C D
O Lord, hear my prayer; O Lord, hear my prayer:
G/B C Am6 B Em Em7/D
when I call, ans - wer me – O Lord, hear my prayer; O
Am/C D Em/G Am B Em Fine
Lord, hear my prayer; come and lis - ten to me. O

ACCOMPANIMENT

Em Em7/D Am/C D G/B C Am6 B Em Em7/D Am/C D Em/G Am B Em
Fine

INSTRUMENTAL PART

(end)

This Taizé chant has travelled throughout the world. It may be appropriate at times to change the text to 'O Lord hear *our* prayer'.

73 ON THE MOUNTAIN

NIGERIA

Words and music: collected Geoff Weaver
arranged Geoff Weaver

Confidently ♩ = 100

G D/A
On the moun - tain, in the val - ley, on the
A7 D D7 G
land and in the sea; on the moun - tain, in the
D/A A7 D
val - ley, on the land and in the sea, hal - le-lu-jah! My

The Igbo Christians of Eastern Nigeria have many short songs of affirmation. This, with words partly drawn from the Psalms, reaffirms God's presence and goodness in all situations.

Poco meno mosso ♩ = 72
Em/G
D/A
God is my por - tion in the land of the liv - ing; my
A7
D
D7
Em/G
God is good for ev - er - more. My God is my por-tion in the
D/A
A7
D
land of the liv - ing; my God is good for ev - er - more.

On the mountain, in the valley,
on the land and in the sea;
on the mountain, in the valley,
on the land and in the sea, hallelujah!

My God is my portion
in the land of the living;
my God is good for evermore.
My God is my portion
in the land of the living;
my God is good for evermore.

74 OUR FATHER WHO IS IN HEAVEN

CARIBBEAN

Words: Lord's Prayer
Music: unknown
arranged David Peacock

Rhythmically ♩ = 108
G D G D
1 Our Fa - ther who is in hea - ven,
2 On earth as it is in hea - ven,
3 For - give us all our tres - pass - es,
(4) lead us not in - to temp - ta - tion,
(5) yours is the king - dom, the power and the glo - ry,
(6) - men, a - men, a - men, a - men,
Em D/F# G
hal - low - èd be your name,
your
give
as
but de -
for
a -
G/B C G D
king - dom come, your will be done,
us this day our dai - ly bread,
we for - give those who tres - pass a - gainst us,
- liv - er us from all that is e - vil,
ev - er and for ev - er,
- men, a - men, a - men, a - men,

This well known Caribbean setting of the Lord's Prayer can be sung very effectively as a solo-response song, with the congregation singing the refrain 'Hallowed be your name', preferably in simple harmonies as suggested.

G
D7
1–5.
G
6.
G
hal-low-èd be your name.
4 And
5 For
6 A-

1 Our Father who is in heaven,
hallowèd be your name,
your kingdom come, your will be done,
hallowèd be your name.

2 On earth as it is in heaven,
hallowèd be your name,
give us this day our daily bread,
hallowèd be your name.

3 Forgive us all our trespasses,
hallowèd be your name,
as we forgive those who trespass against us,
hallowèd be your name.

4 And lead us not into temptation,
hallowèd be your name,
but deliver us from all that is evil,
hallowèd be your name.

5 For yours is the kingdom, the power and the glory,
hallowèd be your name,
for ever and for ever,
hallowèd be your name.

6 Amen, amen, amen, amen,
hallowèd be your name,
amen, amen, amen, amen,
hallowèd be your name.

75 OUVE, SENHOR
Merciful Lord

BRAZIL

Words: S. Monteiro
English: Word & Music
Music: unknown
arranged David Peacock

With expression ♩ = 84

Em
Am7
Ou - ve, Se - nhor, eu es - tou cla - man - do,
Mer - ci - ful Lord, in your lov - ing - kind - ness
D
B7
B7/E
Em
tem pie - da - de de mim e me res - pon - de.
hear our prayer, lis - ten to our in - ter - ces - sion.
Am7/E
Am7
Ou - ve, Se - nhor, eu es - tou cla - man - do,
Mer - ci - ful Lord, in your lov - ing kind ness
D
B7
B7/E
Em
tem pie - da - de de mim e me res - pon - de.
hear our prayer, lis - ten to our in - ter - ces - sion.

An impassioned plea, suitable for times of prayer, in a very Brazilian idiom.

VOCAL HARMONY accompaniment
Sing to 'Ooh' throughout

76 PURIHIN ANG PANGINOON

Give praise to the Lord

PHILIPPINES

Words: from Psalms 149 and 150, F. Ll. Ramirez,
paraphrased Beth Nacion-Puyot and James Minchin
Music: F. Ll. Ramirez
arranged David Peacock

Joyfully 𝅗𝅥. = 52

D A7 Bm D7/A
Pu - ri - hin ang Pa - ngi - no - on, u -
Give praise to the Lord, all the earth, in
G B7 Em G
- ma - wit ng ka - ga - la - kan; at tug - tu -
thank-ful - ness lift up your voice; play your gui -
A7/G D/F# Bm Em7 A
- gin ang gi - ta - ra, at ang ka - a - ya - a - yang li -
- tars to the mu - sic, let the drums keep the rhy - thm a -
F# Bm Em A7 D
Fine
- ra, hi - pan nin - yo ang trom - pe - ta.
- live, with trum - pet and or - gan re - joice.

Like many of the psalms, this song reaffirms the importance of praise and thanksgiving in the midst of troubles. Filipino Christians know a great deal about troubles and burdens, but still manage to sing with great joy and vigor.

Am7 D7 G Em7
1 Sa a - ting pag - ka - ba - ga - bag,
2 Ang pa - sa - ning ma - bi - gat,
3 Ka - ya't Pa - ngin - oo'y ding - gin, and
1 When you are bo - thered by trou - bles,
2 E - ven the loads and the bur - dens
3 We must o - bey God's com - mand - ments,
Am7 D7 G
sa Diyos ta - yo'y tu - ma - wag;
sa 'ting ma - nga ba - li - kat,
lan - das N' - ya'y ta - ha - kin,
seek the Lord's com - fort - ing words:
you find too hea - vy to bear
fol - low the path we are shown;
B♭ C7/B♭ Am7 Dm
sa a - ting ma - nga ka - a - way ta - yo
pi - na - ga - an nang lu - bu - san ng Di -
ha - bam - bu - hay ay pu - ri - hin, ka - ga -
from all your foes you'll be shield - ed, he will
each one is light - ened by Je - sus, the Re -
and ev - ery mo - ment with prais - es we'll pro -
Gm Gm/B♭ Asus A A9 A7
ay Kan-yang i - ni - lig - tas. Pu -
- yos na ta - ga - pag - lig - tas. Pu -
- nda-hang-loob N' - ya sa 'tin. Pu -
al - ways be there for your good. Give
- deem - er and Sav - ior of all. Give
- claim the Lord's deeds to the world. Give

77 QINGCHEN ZAO

God, be praised at early morn

CHINA

Words and music: Da-wei Wang
arranged Geoff Weaver
alternative arrangement Pen-li Chen

Simply ♩ = 92
Capo 1(D)
Eb (D) Cm (Bm) Eb (D) Cm/Eb (Bm) Gm (F#m) Eb/G (D) Cm7 (Bm7)
1 Qing - chen zao qi can - mei Shen, yi - ye ping - an
1 God, be praised at ear - ly morn for pro - tect - ing
Gm (F#m) Cm (Bm) Fm (Em) Bb (A) Eb (D) Fm (Em) Gm (F#m)
meng Shen en, Jin - ri hai qiu Zhu bao -
me at night: on this day, and as I
Cm (Bm) Eb/G (D) Cm (Bm) Gm (F#m) Bb (A) Eb (D)
- you, Wei Zhu zuo - gong xin an - wen.
work, keep me fault - less in your sight.

This song of thanksgiving for safe-keeping is based upon an ancient Chinese folksong.

ALTERNATIVE SETTING

UNISON
1 Qing-chen zao qi can - mei_ Shen, yi - ye_ ping - an
1 God, be_ praised at ear - ly_ morn for pro - tect - ing
meng Shen en, Jin - ri hai qiu Zhu bao -
me_ at night: on this_ day, and as I_
- you, Wei Zhu_ zuo - gong xin an - wen.
work, keep me_ fault - less in your sight.

1 Qingchen zao qi canmei Shen,
yiye pingan meng Shen en,
Jinri hai qiu Zhu baoyou,
Wei Zhu zuogong xin anwen.

2 Shen di rong-guang zhao si-fang,
Chong-man yu-zhou he hui-huang,
zhen guang zhao zai wo xin shang,
Shen en hou ai chang song-yang.

3 Qi-qiu Sheng-ling shi da-neng,
Qu wo zui-i huan xin-ren,
Qian-bei wen-rou xiao-fa Zhu,
Ha-li-lu-ya rong-yao Shen.

1 God, be praised at early morn
for protecting me at night:
on this day, and as I work,
keep me faultless in your sight.

2 God, your glory's radiant beam
fills the universe with grace,
shines its light within my heart –
in your mercy, hear my praise.

3 By your power, O Spirit blessed,
cleanse me from my sins anew;
faithful Master, whom I trust,
let me pledge my love to you.

78 PEOPLE OF FAITH

TAIWAN

Words: I-to Loh
paraphrased James Minchin
Music: Hengchhun melody
arranged I-to Loh

1 Peo - ple of_ faith, by God's com - mand
2 God's light will clear the way_ a - head:
com-fort the_ ex - iles, cap - tives_ free,
up-root and_ pull down what_ is_ wrong,
na-tions con-front with pro - phe - cy:
plant and re - build, and make_ hope_ strong.
such words and deeds re - veal_ God's_ hand.
Go forth with grace your dai - ly_ bread.

79 RABB KI HOWE SANA HAMESHA

Sing the Lord's praises for ever

PAKISTAN

Words: from Psalm 150,
translated Alison Blenkinsop
Music: unknown
arranged Geoff Weaver

Fast and lively ♩ = 126

Capo 3(Bm)
Dm (Bm)
F (D)
Am (F#m)
Rabb-(a) ki ho - we__ sa-na ha-me - sha, rabb-(a) ki ho - we__
Dm (Bm)
Bb (G)
sa - na. ____ Sing the Lord's prai - ses for
F (D)
Am (F#m)
F (D)
Fine
ev-er and ev - er;__ sing the Lord's prai - ses for ev-er. ____

An exuberant Hindi setting of Psalm 150. A performance will be enhanced by the use of rhythmic percussion and echo effects as suggested. Some pronunciation helps are:
Rabb has a little vowel after it – like 'rubber'
ki = key
howe = no way (slight 'v' sound to the 'w')
sana = sun-nah
hamesha = hu-may-sha

Am (F#m)
Dm (Bm)
1 Let us praise the Lord with our voi - ces,
2 Let us praise the Lord in his tem - ple,
3 For he is the might - y cre - a - tor,
C (A)
F (D)
let us praise the Lord with our voi - ces,
let us praise the Lord in his tem - ple,
for he is the might - y cre - a - tor:
Gm (Em)
prais - ing his name for ev - er and ev - er,
thank - ing and prais - ing the Lord for ev - er,
tell of his glo - ry and power for ev - er,
B♭ (G)
F (D)
prais - ing his name for ev - er, ha - me - sha.
thank - ing and prais - ing the Lord, ha - me - sha.
tell of his glo - ry and power, ha - me - sha.

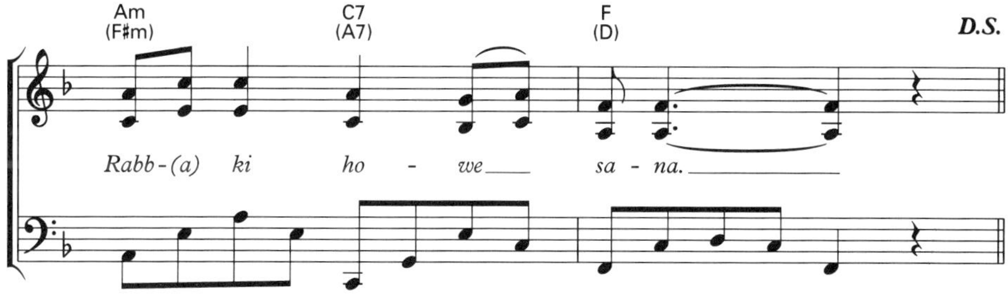

Rabb ki howe sana hamesha,
rabb ki howe sana.
Sing the Lord's praises for ever and ever;
sing the Lord's praises for ever.

1 Let us praise the Lord with our voices,
let us praise the Lord with our voices,
praising his name for ever and ever,
praising his name for ever, *hamesha.*
Rabb ki howe sana.
Sing the Lord's praises

2 Let us praise the Lord in his temple,
let us praise the Lord in his temple,
thanking and praising the Lord for ever,
thanking and praising the Lord, *hamesha.*
Rabb ki howe sana.
Sing the Lord's praises . . .

3 For he is the mighty creator,
for he is the mighty creator:
tell of his glory and power for ever,
tell of his glory and power, *hamesha.*
Rabb ki howe sana.
Sing the Lord's praises . . .

4 Loudly play the horns and the trumpets,
loudly play the horns and the trumpets;
play on the lute and the pipes together,
play on the lute and the pipes, *hamesha.*
Rabb ki howe sana.
Sing the Lord's praises . . .

5 Play with skill the violin and 'cello,
play with skill the violin and 'cello;
rattle the tambourine and drums together,
rattle the tambourine and drums, *hamesha.*
Rabb ki howe sana.
Sing the Lord's praises . . .

6 Play the flute so sweet and melodious,
play the flute so sweet and melodious;
clashing the cymbals and gongs together,
clashing the cymbals together, *hamesha.*
Rabb ki howe sana.
Sing the Lord's praises . . .

7 Everybody clap hands together,
everybody clap hands together;
sing the Lord's praises for ever and ever,
sing the Lord's praises for ever, *hamesha.*
Rabb ki howe sana.
Sing the Lord's praises . . .

80 SANNA

SOUTH AFRICA

Words: traditional
Music: unknown
arranged Geoff Weaver

Joyfully ♩ = 100

C G F C
San-na, san-na-ni-na, san-na, san-na, san-na.
(- na)
SOLO Ho - san - na, san -
G F C G7
San-na, san-na-ni-na, san-na, san-na, san-na.
SOLO Ho - san-na
San - na, san-na, san-
C C/G G7 C G7
- na san-na-ni-na, san-na, san-na, san-na.
SOLO Ho - san-na
San - na, san-na, san-
repeats
last time
C C/G G7 C D.C. C
- na san-na-ni-na, san-na, san-na, san-na.
- na.
SOLO Ho - san-na, san -

Sanna is a shortened form of *Hosanna*. It is very effective to start this song quietly, as if in a distant procession, and then to get louder and more exuberant as the imaginary procession draws nearer.

81 STAND, O STAND FIRM

CAMEROON

Words: traditional
Music: traditional
arranged John L Bell

Confidently
ALL Stand, O stand firm; stand, O
stand firm; stand, O stand firm and see what the Lord can do.
div.
Fine
LEADER Oh my sis - ters, stand ve - ry firm.

ALL
Stand, O stand firm;
stand, O stand firm;
stand, O stand firm
and see what the Lord can do.

LEADER
Oh my sisters, stand very firm . . .
Oh my brothers, stand very firm . . .
All you children, stand very firm . . .
All you elders, stand very firm . . .
Let God's people stand very firm . . .
or
Let the hungry folk stand very firm . . .
Let the victimized stand very firm . . .
Let the peacemakers stand very firm . . .
etc.

This is a great song of solidarity. It has been used to encourage people dispossessed of their land to keep protesting. It has been used as a song of encouragement to the recently baptised. All that is to be required is for the congregation to know the chorus and for the leader to compose or improvise calls appropriate to the occasion.

82 SANTO, SANTO

Holy, holy

ARGENTINA

Words and music: unknown
arranged Geoff Weaver

Worshipfully ♩ = 84
C G6 Dm6/B Am F Cmaj7/F F
San - to, san - to, san - to, mí co - ra - zón te a -
Ho - ly, ho - ly, ho - ly, my heart, my heart a -
F/C C F G
- do - ra! Mí co - ra - zón te
- dores you! My heart is glad to
C Em/B Am Dm7 G7 F/G C
sabe de - cir: san - to eres Se - ñor.
say the words: you are ho - ly, Lord.

This heart-felt love song may be sung in unison, in two parts, or in rich harmony.

Santo, santo, santo,
mí corazón te adora!
Mí corazón te sabe decir:
santo eres Señor.

Holy, holy, holy,
my heart, my heart adores you!
My heart is glad to say the words:
you are holy, Lord.

INSTRUMENTAL OBLIGATO

Oboe

Flute

B♭ Clarinet

Simple part

83 SANTO, SANTO, SANTO

Holy, holy, holy is the Lord

El Salvador

Words: unknown
English adaptation, Word & Music
Music: unknown
arranged Christopher Norton

♩. = 108

Capo 3(D)
F (D) B♭ (G) F (D) C7 (A7) F (D)
B♭ (G) F (D) B♭ (G) C (A) F (D)
F (D)
San-to, san - to, san - to, san - to, san-to,
Ho-ly, ho - ly, ho - ly, ho - ly, ho-ly,
C7 (A7)
san - toes nues - tro Dios, Se - ñor de to - da la tie - rra, san-to,
ho - ly is our God; God, the Lord of earth and hea - ven, ho ly,
F (D)
san - toes nues - tro Dios. San-to, san - to, san - to, san - to, san-to,
ho - ly is our God. Ho-ly, ho - ly, ho - ly, ho - ly, ho-ly,

This extract from the *Missa Popular Salvadorena,* with its characteristic folk dance alternation of 6/8 and 3/4 time, needs a lively rhythmic accompaniment (percussion and guitars) and a radiant abandon on the part of the congregation.

C7 (A7)
san - toes nues - tro Dios, Se - ñor de to - da la his - to - ria, san - to,
ho - ly is our God; God, the Lord of all of his - tory, ho - ly,
F (D) Fine F (D) B♭ (G)
san - toes nues - tro Dios. Que a com - pa - ña a nues - tro pue - blo, que
ho - ly is our God. Who walks be - side __ our peo - ple, who
C (A) F (D) B♭ (G) C (A)
vi - ve en nues - tras lu - chas, del u - ni - ver - so en - te - ro el ú - ni - co Se -
helps us in our strug - gle? In ev - ery land and na - tion our one sav - ior is
F (D) B♭ (G) C (A)
- ñor. Ben - di - tos los que en su nom - bre el E - van - ge - lio a -
God! Tell all the peo - ple that he is Lord, preach the Gos - pel,
D.C. al Fine
F (D) B♭ (G) C (A) F (D)
- nun - cian, la bue - na y gran no - ti - cia de la li - be - ra - ción.
bring good news; he has sent us to pro - claim new free - dom and peace!

84 SARANAM, SARANAM

Jesus, Savior, Lord

PAKISTAN

Words: from Psalm 61
after D. T. Niles
Music: Punjabi melody
arranged Geoff Weaver

With feeling ♩ = 88
Capo 1(D)
Eb (D) Bb7 (A7) Eb (D)
Sa - ra - nam, sa - ra - nam, sa - ra - nam,
Eb (D) Ab (G) Eb (D)
Je - sus, Sav - ior, Lord, now to you I come, Sa - ra -
Bb7 (A7) Eb (D) Ab (G)
- nam, sa - ra-nam, sa - ra - nam; you my Rock, my re - fuge, my
Eb (D) Bb7 (A7) Eb (D)
Fine
hea - venly home, Sa - ra - nam, sa - ra-nam, sa - ra - nam.

A hymn much loved by Christians from the Indian subcontinent, based on words by D. T. Niles and set to a Punjabi melody. 'Saranam' means 'refuge' or 'I take refuge'.

A♭ (G)
E♭ (D)
B♭7/D (A7)
B♭
1 From the earth wher-ev-er I may be, out of des - pe - ra - tion and through
2 In your heart give me a hid - ing place, and be - neath your wings let me find
E♭ (D)
E♭7
A♭ (G)
a - go - ny, I cry in help - less - ness – O
shel - tering grace; O let me see the sun - shine
E♭ (D)
B♭7 (A7)
E♭ (D)
D.S.
ans - wer me,
of your face,
Sa - ra - nam, sa - ra - nam, sa - ra - nam.

3 Then with joy to you my vows I'll pay,
and give thanks for all your mercy every day;
I'll humbly follow in your perfect way,
Saranam, saranam, saranam.
Jesus, Savior . . .

4 Glory to the Father and the Son,
with the Holy Spirit ever Three-in-One;
we'll sing in heaven praises here begun,
Saranam, saranam, saranam.
Jesus, Savior . . .

85 SENT BY THE LORD AM I

NICARAGUA

Words: from the oral tradition
translation Jorge Maldonodo
Music: traditional
arranged David Peacock

Confidently ♩ = 100

Capo 3(Dm)
Fm (Dm)
Sent by the Lord am I; my hands are rea-dy now to
Bbm/G (Gm)
C (A)
Fm (Dm)
make the earth the place in which the king-dom comes. Sent
HARMONY
by the Lord am I; my hands are rea - dy now to
Bbm/G (Gm)
C (A)
Fm (Dm)
make the earth the place in which the king-dom comes. The

A song from the folk tradition of Nicaragua. The use of the minor key somehow adds strength and resolve to the commitment to Christ's mission.

UNISON
Bbm7 (Gm7)
Eb (C)
Abmaj7 (F)
Dbmaj7 (Bb)
an - gels can - not change a world of hurt and pain in -
Bbm/G (Gm)
C (A)
F (D)
F/A
- to a world of love, of jus - tice and of peace. The
HARMONY
Bbm7 (Gm7)
Eb (C)
Abmaj7 (F)
Dbmaj7 (Bb)
task is mine to do, to set it real - ly free. Oh,
Bbm/G (Gm)
C (A)
F (D)
help me to o - bey; help me to do your will.

Sent by the Lord am I;
my hands are ready now
to make the earth the place
in which the kingdom comes.
Sent by the Lord am I;
my hands are ready now
to make the earth the place
in which the kingdom comes.

The angels cannot change
a world of hurt and pain
into a world of love,
of justice and of peace.
The task is mine to do,
to set it really free.
Oh, help me to obey;
help me to do your will.

86 SING OF HIS VICTORY

EGYPT

Words: from Revelation 4 & 5
Word & Music
Music: unknown
arranged Geoff Weaver

Gently ♩. = 69
Capo 1(Bm)
Cm (Bm) Fm (Em) G7 (F#7) Cm (Bm)
1 Sing of his vic - to-ry, tell of his sac - ri-fice:
2 Je - sus, you died for us, pur - chased our li - ber-ty,
A♭ (G) Bdim (B♭dim) G7 (F#7) C (B)
wor - thy the Lamb of God who shall re-ceive our love!
made us a priest - ly king-dom, fit to serve our God:
Fm (Em) Cm (Bm)
Let ev - ery crea - ture bring true praise to wor - ship him –
from all hu-ma - ni - ty, now to your glo - ry be
G (F#) Fm6/D (Em) G7 (F#7) Cm (Bm)
hon - or and wis - dom and power for ev - er-more.
hon - or and wis - dom and power for ev - er-more!

The ancient Egyptian Coptic Church is rich in history and tradition. Its liturgy is elaborate and colorful, but there is also a place for simple songs from the heart, such as this item of praise. This is most effective as a solo.

Chorus

Cm (Bm) Ab (G) Bb (A) Gm (F#m)
Je - sus, our sav - ior, you have re-deemed us,
Ab (G) Fm (Em) G (F#) Ab (G) G (F#)
made us the roy - al priest - hood of God:
Cm (Bm) Fm (Em) Bb (A) Eb (D) Cm (Bm)
from ev - ery na - tion where you have called us,
Ab (G) Fm (Em) G (F#) F/G (E) G (F#) Cm (Bm)
praise – al - le - lu - ia! Glo - ry – A - men!

87 SIYAHAMBA

We are marching

SOUTH AFRICA

Words: African origin
collected and edited by Anders Nyberg
English verses 2 and 3: Andrew Maries
Music: African melody scored by
Notman KB, Ljungsbro and Lars Parkman

Joyfully ♩ = 120
G
C
Si - ya - hamb' e - ku - kha - nye - ni 'kwen - khos, si - ya -
1.
2.
D
G
'kwen - khos,
- hamb' e - ku - kha - nye - ni 'kwen - khos,
si - ya - hamb' e - ku - kha - nye - ni 'kwen (kha -
G7
hamb - ba
- nye - ni 'kwen - khos). Si - ya - ham - ba (ham - ba, si - ya -
Oo
Si - ya
- ham - ba, ham - ba), si - ya - hamb' e - ku - kha - nye - ni 'kwen - khos.

An exuberant song of hope from South Africa which has become popular in recent years. Experiment with variations in the harmony. It is hard to stand still while singing this song!

Joyfully ♩ = 120
G C
We are march - ing in the light of God, we are
1. 2.
D G D G
God
march ing in the light of God, we are march-ing in the light of, (the
G7 C
we are march - ing
light of God). We are march-ing, (march-ing, we are
G C D G
Oh, we are
march-ing, march-ing,) we are march-ing in the light of God!

OPTIONAL FURTHER VERSES

2 We are living in the love of God . . .

3 We are moving in the power of God . . .

88 SIZOHAMBA NAYE

We are on the Lord's road

SOUTH AFRICA

Words and music: unknown

Lively ♩ = 63

Capo 3(D)
F (D)
1 Si - zo-ham-ba na - ye (wo)
1 We are on the Lord's road, (wo)
C (A)
F (D)
(wo) si - zo-ham-ba na - ye
(wo) we are on the Lord's road,
B♭ (G)
Gm (Em)
F (D)
Dm (Bm)
C7 (A7)
F (D)
ngo-mhla wen - ja - bu - la si - zo - ham - ba na - ye
on our way to hea - ven – we are on the Lord's road,
B♭ (G)
Gm (Em)
F (D)
Dm (Bm)
C7 (A7)
F (D)
ngo-mhla wen - ja - bu - la si - zo - ham - ba na - ye.
on our way to hea - ven – we are on the Lord's road.

A lively song from South Africa. Try and feel the rhythms as exactly as possible.

1 *Sizohamba naye (wo) sizohamba naye*
Sizohamba naye . . .
ngomhla wenjabula
sizohamba naye
ngomhla wenjabula
sizohamba naye.

2 *Sizohalalisa (wo) sizohalalisa*
sizohalalisa . . .
ngomhla wenjabula
sizohalalisa naye
ngomhla wenjabula
sizohalalisa naye.

3 *Sizohlabelela (wo) sizohlabelela*
sizohlabelela . . .
ngomhla wenjabula
sizohlabelela naye
ngomhla wenjabula
sizohlabelela naye.

1 We are on the Lord's road,
we are on the Lord's road,
we are on the Lord's road,
we are on the Lord's road,
on our way to heaven –
we are on the Lord's road,
on our way to heaven –
we are on the Lord's road.

2 We shall sing the Lord's praise,
we shall sing the Lord's praise,
we shall sing the Lord's praise,
we shall sing the Lord's praise,
on our way to heaven –
we shall sing the Lord's praise,
on our way to heaven –
we shall sing the Lord's praise.

3 We shall live the Lord's word,
we shall live the Lord's word,
we shall live the Lord's word,
we shall live the Lord's word,
on our way to heaven –
we shall live the Lord's word,
on our way to heaven –
we shall live the Lord's word.

4 Hallelujah, amen,
hallelujah, amen,
hallelujah, amen,
hallelujah, amen,
on our way to heaven –
hallelujah, amen,
on our way to heaven –
hallelujah, amen.

89 TAMA NGAKAU

Lord of love

NEW ZEALAND

Words: from Romans 3:21–26
traditional Maori, paraphrased Michael Perry
Music: Maori traditional melody
arranged Geoff Weaver

With expression ♩ = 50
G D7 Em C G D7
1 Ta - ma nga - kau ma - ri - e, ta - ma
1 Lord of love, you come to bless all who
G D7/G G D/F# Em C
a T'a - tu - a, te - nei to - nu
will by faith con - fess Je - sus, God's own
G * Bm Am/C Em/B Am7 D7 G
ma - tou, a - ro - hai - na mai.
right - eous - ness to the world made known.

A simple prayer, based on a traditional Maori melody, most effective when sung unaccompanied.

*ALTERNATIVE ENDING

G D7 G/D D7 G
- tou, a - ro - hai - na mai.
- ness to the world made known.

1 *Tama ngakau marie,*
tama a T'atua,
tenei tonu matou,
arohaina mai.

2 *Murua ra nga hara:*
woto hina mai,
enei here kino,
whakararu nei.

3 *Homai he aroha*
mou i mate nei
tenei ra, e Ihu
tukina e koe.

1 Lord of love, you come to bless
all who will by faith confess
Jesus, God's own righteousness
to the world made known.

2 Bruised on Calvary's weary road,
bowed beneath the curse of God,
shedding the atoning blood
sacrifice is done.

3 By the arms you open wide,
by your wounded hands and side,
Jesus, we are justified,
saved by grace alone!

90

TATA POKELELA

Everything is yours, Lord

ZAMBIA

Words: from 1 Chronicles 29, unknown
English: Word & Music
Music: unknown
arranged Geoff Weaver

Joyfully ♩ = 132

LEADER
D G D
Ta - ta po - ke - le - la If - ya - bu - pe fye - su,
Ev - ery-thing is yours, Lord; ev - ery-thing comes from you:
D/A A7 D
If - yo twa - mi pe - la le - lo.
all we have we of - fer to you.

An offertory song, in leader-response format. Improvised percussion accompaniment will help to give something of the flavor of the offertory, which in African worship is so often an exuberant (and extended!) experience.

ALL
G D A7 D7
Po - ke - le - le - ni ta - ta,
Ac - cept our love, Lord, we pray;
G D/A A7 D
Po - ke - le - le - ni le - lo.
re - ceive our gifts, Lord, to - day.

91 TATANACA, MAMANACA, SARANTAÑANI

Men and women, let us walk

Bolivia

Words and music: Zoilo Yanapa
arranged Christopher Norton

Brightly ♩ = 72
Capo 3(Bm)
Dm (Bm) Gm7 (Em7) C7 (A7) F (D)
1 Ta - ta - na - ca, ma - ma - na - ca, Sa - ran - ta - ña - ni!
(2) Igle - sia na - ca - sa - ja ma - ya-ghasi-ña - ni,
1 Men and wo - men, let us walk, and let's walk to - ge - ther;
(2) Church be one strong bo - dy, walk-ing to - ge - ther;
Dm (Bm) Gm7 (Em7) C7 (A7) F (D)
Ta - ta - na - ca, ma - ma - na - ca, Sa - ran - ta - ña - ni! Way - na -
ta - ke Igle - sia na - ca - sa - ja ma - ya-ghasi-ña - ni. Ma - ya -
men and wo - men, let us walk, and let's walk to - ge - ther. Bro-thers,
let the Church be one strong bo - dy, walk-ing to - ge - ther. Ev - ery
Gm7 (Em7) Dm/A (Bm) A7#5 (F#7) Dm (Bm)
- na - ka, ta - wa - co - na - ka, sayt' a - si - ña - ni. Way - na -
- qui, ta - ke - ni, Sa - ran - ta - ña - ni. Ma - ya -
sis - ters, child - ren and youth, let's all move to - ge - ther; bro-thers,
mem-ber touched by each o - ther, keep-ing to - ge - ther; ev - ery

This dance-song comes from the Aymara people of Bolivia. With such vitality in their worship, it is not surprising that they are part of the fastest growing church in their country.

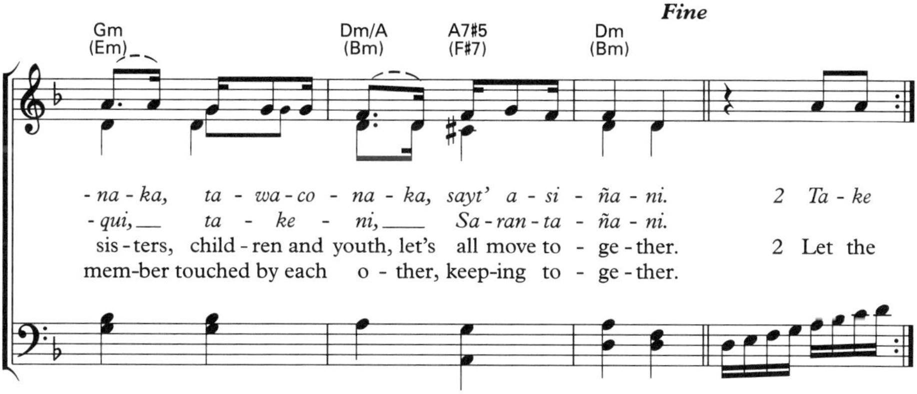
Fine
Gm (Em)
Dm/A (Bm)
A7♯5 (F♯7)
Dm (Bm)
-na - ka, ta - wa - co - na - ka, sayt' a - si - ña - ni. 2 Ta - ke
-qui, ta - ke - ni, Sa - ran - ta - ña - ni.
sis - ters, child - ren and youth, let's all move to - ge - ther. 2 Let the
mem-ber touched by each o - ther, keep-ing to - ge - ther.

1 *Tatanaca, mamanaca, Sarantañani!*
Tatanaca, mamanaca, Sarantañani!
Waynanaka, tawaconaka, sayt' asiñani.
Waynanaka, tawaconaka, sayt' asiñani.

2 *Take Iglesia nacasaja mayaghasiñani,*
take Iglesia nacasaja mayaghasiñani.
Mayaqui, takeni, Sarantañani.
Mayaqui, takeni, Sarantañani.

1 Men and women, let us walk,
and let's walk together;
men and women, let us walk,
and let's walk together.
Brothers, sisters, children and youth,
let's all move together;
brothers, sisters, children and youth,
let's all move together.

2 Let the Church be one strong body,
walking together;
let the Church be one strong body,
walking together.
Every member touched by each other,
keeping together;
every member touched by each other,
keeping together.

92 TE AMO

I love you

ARGENTINA

Words and music: unknown
arranged David Peacock

Unhurried ♩ = 80

D A/C#
Te a - mo, te a - mo es
I love you, I love you – the
G/B Em7 G/A A7
to - do lo que pue - do de - cir. Te a -
earth and hea - ven show forth your ways. I
D Bm7 Em7 D/F#
- do - ro, te a - do - ro, to - do mi ser con - fi - a en
love you, I love you; with all my heart I sing out your
Em/A C/D G A9/G
ti. Yo te a - ma - ré y te a -
praise. I praise you, Lord, yes, I

An expressive worship song which is sung throughout Latin America.

F♯m Bm7 Em7 Em7/D
-do-ra-ré no im-por-ta lo que pue-da ve-
praise you, Lord, for ev-ery gift and true joy you
C A7 G A9/G
-nir. En ti Señ-or siem-pre
send; I love you, Lord, yes, I
F♯m Bm7 Em7 G/A A7 D
con-fia-ré y te a-ma-ré has-ta el fin.
love you, Lord, and I will love you to the end.

Te amo, te amo
es todo lo que puedo decir.
Te adoro, te adoro,
todo mi ser confía en ti.

Yo te amaré y te adoraré
no importa lo que pueda venir.
En ti Señor siempre confiaré
y te amaré hasta el fin.

I love you, I love you –
the earth and heaven show forth your ways.
I love you, I love you;
with all my heart I sing out your praise.

I praise you, Lord, yes, I praise you, Lord,
for every gift and true joy you send;
I love you, Lord, yes, I love you, Lord,
and I will love you to the end.

93 TERI ARADHANA KARU

Lord, in your mercy, remember me

INDIA

Words: after the Indian song
from Psalm 25, Word & Music
Music: unknown
arranged Geoff Weaver

Expressively ♩ = 108
Dm
Te - ri a - ra - dha - na ka - ru
Lord, in your mer - cy, re - mem - ber me,
Gm
Te - ri a - ra - dha - na ka - ru
Lord, in your mer - cy, re - mem - ber me;
A7 Dm B♭ Gm
Pa - pa - ksha - ma ker jee - van de - dey
show me your ways, Lord, guide me in your truth and teach me, Lord:

This is only the refrain of a much longer song originally in Hindi, and sung as a morning prayer. Its character is perhaps best expressed by a solo female voice, as the arranger first heard it hauntingly sung by a young Indian woman.

G#dim Dm/A A7
da - ya - ki ya - cha - na ka - ru.
you are my God, my king, my sav - ior.
Ped.
Dm Dm
Te - ri a - ra - dha - na ka - ru.
Lord, in your mer - cy, re - mem - ber me.
Te - ri a - ra - dha - na ka - ru.
Lord, in your mer - cy, re - mem - ber me.

Teri aradhana karu
Teri aradhana karu
Papakshama ker jeevan dedey
dayaki yachana karu.

Teri aradhana karu.
Teri aradhana karu.

Lord, in your mercy, remember me,
Lord, in your mercy, remember me;
show me your ways, Lord,
guide me in your truth and teach me, Lord:
you are my God, my king, my savior.

Lord, in your mercy, remember me.
Lord, in your mercy, remember me.

94 THE LORD IS MY LIGHT

CZECHOSLOVAKIA

Words: from Psalm 27
paraphrased John L. Bell
Music: Czech hymn tune
arranged Geoff Weaver

Confidently ♩ = 138

1 The Lord___ is my light, my light and
2 Should e - vil powers ad - vance, should arm - ies
3 One thing I ask the Lord. This on - ly
4 Pre - served by God from harm, se - cure in

my sal - va - tion. With God pro - tect - ing me
try to kill,___ let them sur - round me and
I de - sire:___ al - ways in wor - ship to
him a - lone,___ I will re - joice in the

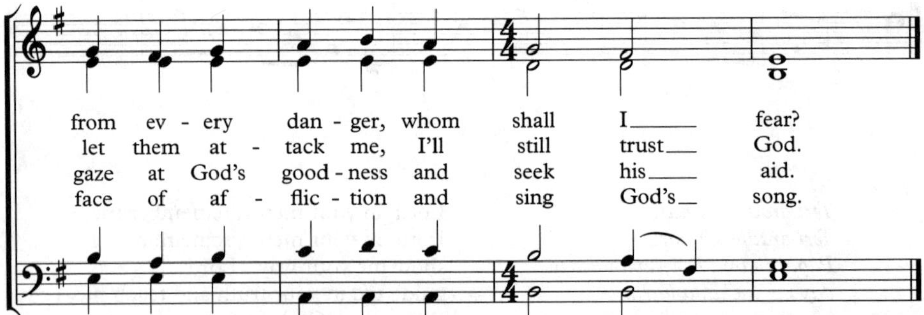

from ev - ery dan - ger, whom shall I___ fear?
let them at - tack me, I'll still trust___ God.
gaze at God's good - ness and seek his___ aid.
face of af - flic - tion and sing God's___ song.

A setting of Psalm 27 based on a 17th century Czech hymn tune and sung, among others, by the Evangelical Church of the Czech Brethren. The minor mode gives it a strength and seriousness of purpose. It can be sung either in parts or in unison with keyboard accompaniment.

95 THE MOST EXCELLENCY IS JESUS

NIGERIA

Words: unknown
collected Geoff Weaver
Music: unknown
arranged Geoff Weaver

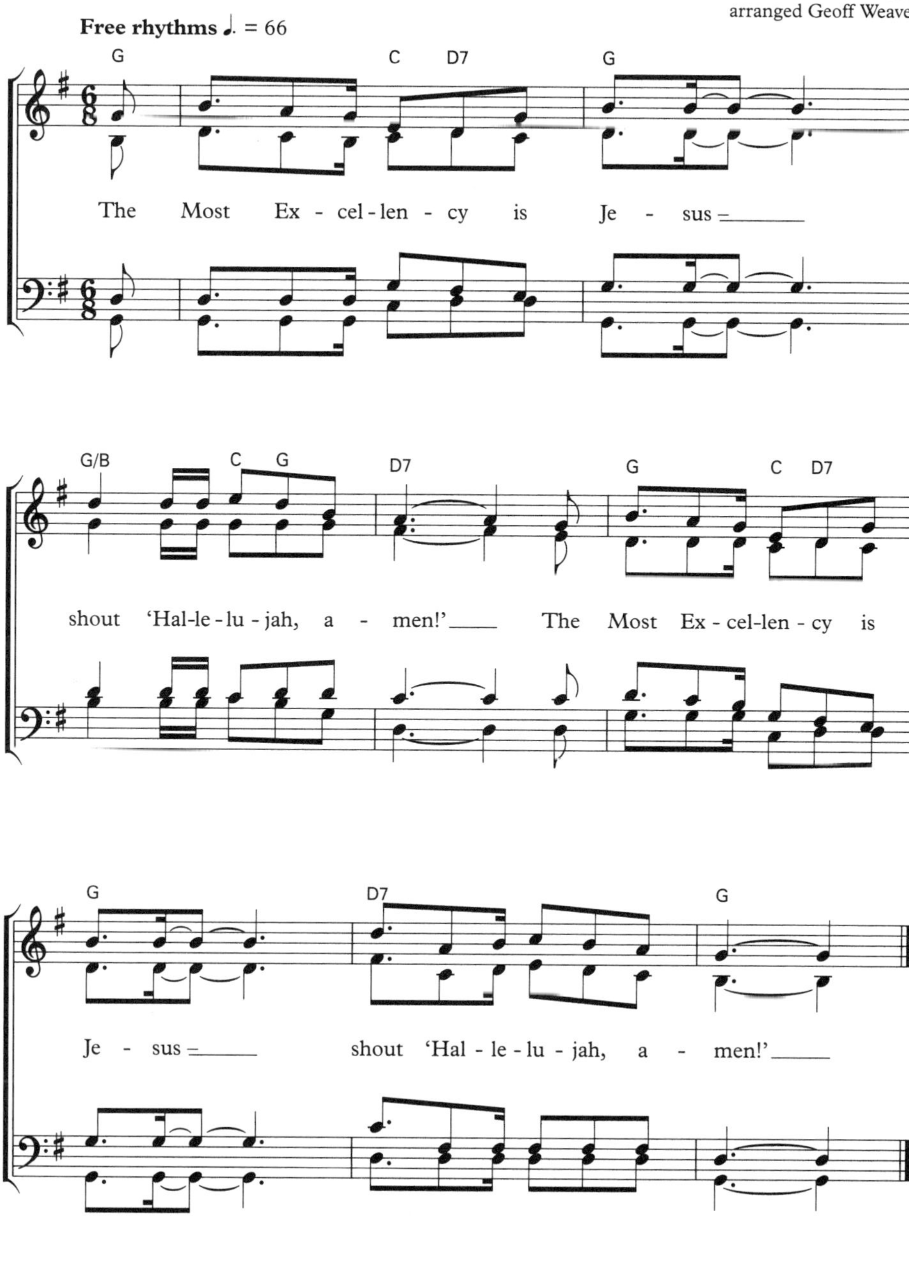
Free rhythms ♩. = 66
G C D7 G
The Most Ex - cel - len - cy is Je - sus –
G/B C G D7 G C D7
shout 'Hal-le - lu - jah, a - men!' The Most Ex - cel-len - cy is
G D7 G
Je - sus – shout 'Hal - le - lu - jah, a - men!'

The arranger had some difficulty in notating this song in Kano Cathedral, Nigeria, largely due to the complex, intuitive rhythms. Feel them, rather than trying to count them!

96 THE PEACE OF THE EARTH

GUATEMALA

Words: traditional, translated Christine Carson
Music: Guatemalan traditional melody
arranged John L Bell

Gently

The peace of the earth be with you, the peace of the hea - vens
too; the peace of the riv - ers be with you, the
peace of the o-ceans too. Deep peace fall-ing ov - er
Deep peace, deep peace fall-ing ov - er
you; God's peace grow - ing in you.
you; God's peace, God's peace grow - ing in you.

This beautiful blessing song that may be sung once or repeatedly as members of the congregation bless each other when they leave.

97 THUMA MINA

Send me, Lord

SOUTH AFRICA

Words: African origin,
collected and edited by Anders Nyberg
Music: African melody scored by Notman KB,
Ljungsbro and Lars Parkman

Worshipfully ♩ = 100

E B C#m B E C#m E
LEADER
Thu - ma mi-na,
Send me, Lord:
ALL
Thu-ma mi-na thu - ma mi - na thu-ma
Send me, Je-sus, send me, Je - sus, send me,
to repeat
to end
F#m E/B B E B E
thu - ma mi - na
send me, Lord.
mi - na, so - man - dla. Thu-ma - dla.
Je - sus, send me, Lord. Send me, Lord.

LEADER	*Thuma mina,*	1	LEADER	Send me, Lord:
ALL	*thuma mina*		ALL	Send me, Jesus,
	thuma mina			send me, Jesus,
	thuma mina,			send me, Jesus,
	somandla.			send me, Lord.
		2	LEADER	Lead me, Lord:
			ALL	Lead me, Jesus . . .
		3	LEADER	Fill me, Lord:
			ALL	Fill me, Jesus . . .

This text comes from the rich South African tradition of sacred song which is noted for its harmonies and for its strength and dignity. Sing this song unaccompanied and use it in a variety of ways, e.g. after intercessions, after a talk, at the end of the service.

98 TOUT EST FAIT POUR LA GLOIRE DE DIEU

All is made for the glory of God

CAMEROON

Words and music: Abel Nkuinji
arranged Geoff Weaver

Rhythmic ♩ = 138

Capo 3(D)
F (D)
Bb (G)
F (D)
F7
1 Tout est fait pour la gloi - re de Dieu. A -
1 All is made for the glo - ry of God. A -
Bb (G)
Bb6
F (D)
- men, (A - men) a - men! Tout est fait pour la
- men, (A - men) a - men! All is made for the
SOLO Al - le - lu - ia
Al - le - lu - ia
Bb (G)
F (D)
F7
Bb (G)
Bb6
F (D)
F7
gloi - re de Dieu. A - men, (A - men) a - men, a - men, a -
glo - ry of God. A - men, (A - men) a - men, a - men, a -

A lively rhythmic song from French-speaking West Africa. It can be extended indefinitely, as is the practice in Africa, by naming other subjects and creatures which exist for God's glory.

B♭ (G)
F (D)
-men, (A-men) a - men! (A-men!) Tout est fait pour la
-men, (A-men) a - men! (A-men!) All is made for the
B♭ (G) F (D) F7 B♭ (G) F (D)
gloi-re de Dieu. A - men, (A-men) a - men!
glo-ry of God. A - men, (A-men) a - men!

1 Tout est fait pour la gloire de Dieu.
Amen, amen!
Tout est fait pour la gloire de Dieu.
Amen, amen, amen, amen, amen!
Tout est fait pour la gloire de Dieu.
Amen, amen!

2 La vie c'est pour la gloire de Dieu . . .

3 Le culte est pour la gloire de Dieu . . .

1 All is made for the glory of God.
Amen, amen!
All is made for the glory of God.
Amen, amen, amen, amen, amen!
All is made for the glory of God.
Amen, amen!

2 Living is for the glory of God . . .

3 Worship is for the glory of God . . .

99 TY WYZWOLILES NAS (ABBA OJCZE)

Brothers and sisters

POLAND

Words: J. Góra
English: Word & Music
Music: J. Sykulski
arranged Geoff Weaver

Lively with majesty ♩ = 112

C F C
1 Ty wyz - wo - li - les nas, Pa - nie
2 Bo Kos - ci‿ol jak drz - e - wo zyc - ia w wie -
1 Bro - thers and sis - ters, of God we sing, the
2 Bro - thers and sis - ters, of Christ we sing, the
C/E F/A G7sus G7 C E7/B
z kaj - dan i sa - mych sie - bie, a Chrys - tus sta - jac sie
- czno - sci za - pu - sz - cza kor - ze - nie prze - ni - ka nas - za cod -
Fa - ther who has made us all. O God, we give you the
Sav - ior who re - deemed us all. O God, we give you the
Am/C E/B Am F C/E F/A G7sus G
bra - tem na - uczyl nas wo - lac do Cie - bie:
- zien - nosc i po - ka - zu - je nam Cie - bie.
glo - ry, we give you the praise and the glo - ry:
glo - ry, we give you the praise and the glo - ry:

This song, which has become popular in ecumenical gatherings, breathes the joy in new-found freedom, in all its aspects, which Christians from Eastern Europe understand well. It should be strongly rhythmic, and has something of the character of a march. When using the English version, '*Abba Ojcze*' (pronounced '*Oi-chay*') may be substituted at the end of each verse.

C F/C C G7 C F C G
Ab - ba – Oj - cze! Ab - ba – Oj - cze!
Ab - ba, Fa - ther. Ab - ba, Fa - ther.
C/E E7 Am F C/G G7 C
Ab - ba – Oj - cze! Ab-ba – Oj - cze!
Ab - ba, Fa - ther. Ab-ba, Fa - ther.

1 *Ty wyzwoliles nas, Panie*
z kajdan i samych siebie,
a Chrystus stajac sie bratem
nauczyl nas wolac do Ciebie:
Abba – Ojcze! Abba – Ojcze!
Abba – Ojcze! Abba – Ojcze!

2 *Bo Kosciol jak drzewo zycia*
w wiecznosci zapuszcza korzenie
przenika nasza codziennosc
i pokazuje nam Ciebie.
Abba – Ojcze . . .

3 *Bog hojnym Dawca jest zycia*
On wyswobodzil nas z smierci
i przygarniajac do siebie
uczynil swoimi dziecmi.
Abba – Ojcze . . .

4 *Wszyscy jestesmy bracmi*
jestesmy jedna rodzina.
Tej prawdy nic juz nie zacmi
i teraz jest jej godzina.
Abba – Ojcze . . .

1 Brothers and sisters, of God we sing,
the Father who has made us all.
O God, we give you the glory,
we give you the praise and the glory:
Abba, Father. Abba, Father.
Abba, Father. Abba, Father.

2 Brothers and sisters, of Christ we sing,
the Savior who redeemed us all.
O God, we give you the glory,
we give you the praise and the glory:
Abba, Father . . .

3 Brothers and sisters, of power we sing,
the Spirit who empowers us all.
O God, we give you the glory,
we give you the praise and the glory:
Abba, Father . . .

4 Brothers and sisters, to God we sing,
to Father, Son and Spirit – all.
O God, we give you the glory,
we give you the praise and the glory:
Abba, Father . . .

100 VEM, JESUS NOSSA ESPERANÇA

Come to be our hope, Lord Jesus

BRAZIL

Words: Jorge Rodríguez
Jaci C. Maraschin
Music: Marcilide de Oliveira Filko
arranged Christopher Norton

Rhythmically ♩ = 120

Capo 1(D)
E♭ (D) D♭ (C) E♭ (D) A♭7 (G7) B♭7 (A7)
1 Vem, Je - sus nos - sa es - pe - ran - ça nos - sas vi - das li - ber -
2 Vem te - cer um mun - do no - vo nos cam - in - hos de verd - a -
1 Come to be our hope, Lord Je - sus, come to set our peo - ple
2 Come to build your new cre - a - tion through the road of ser - vant -
E♭ (D) D♭ (C) E♭ (D)
- tar. Vem, nas - cer em nós, cri - an - ça vem o
- de; pa - ra que, a - fi - nal, o po - vo vi - va em
free; from op - pres - sion come, re - lease us, turn de -
- hood; give new life to ev - ery na - tion, chang - ing
A♭7 (G7) B♭7 (A7) E♭ (D) A♭ (G) B♭ (A)
teu po - der nos dar. Vem, li - ber - ta os pri - sio -
ple - na li - berd - ade. Vem, Je - sus, a - bre o fu -
- feat to vic - to - ry! Come, re - lease from ev - ery
e - vil in - to good. Come and o - pen our to -

Jaci Maraschin is one of Brazil's foremost Church composers. For him the dance finds its place in worship reflecting hope, while the flattened third portrays the pain of oppression. A light rhythmic accompaniment helps to bring out the dance-like character here.

Eb (D) Fm/Ab (Em) G7 (F#7) Cm (Bm) Eb7 (D7)
-nei - ros da in - jus - ti - ça e da a - fli - ção; vem, re -
-tu - ro do teu reino de a - leg - ri - a. Vem, der -
pri - son those who suf - fer in our land: in your
-mor - row for a king - dom now so near; take a -
Ab (G) Bb (A) Eb (D) Cb (Bb) Ab (G) Bb (A) Eb (D)
-ú - ne os bra - si lei - ros em a - mor e em com-preen-são.
-ruba o i-men - so mu - ro que se - para a noite e o dia.
love we find the rea-son still to live and un - der-stand.
-way all hu - man sor-row – give us hope in place of fear.

1 *Vem, Jesus nossa esperança*
nossas vidas libertar.
Vem, nascer em nós, criança
vem o teu poder nos dar.
Vem, liberta os prisioneiros
da injustiça e da aflição;
vem, reúne os brasi leiros
em amor e em compreensão.

2 *Vem tecer um mundo novo*
nos caminhos de verdade;
para que, afinal, o povo
viva em plena liberdade.
Vem, Jesus, abre o futuro
do teu reino de alegria.
Vem, derruba o imenso muro
que separa a noite e o dia.

1 Come to be our hope, Lord Jesus,
come to set our people free;
from oppression come, release us,
turn defeat to victory!
Come, release from every prison
those who suffer in our land:
in your love we find the reason
still to live and understand.

2 Come to build your new creation
through the road of servanthood;
give new life to every nation,
changing evil into good.
Come and open our tomorrow
for a kingdom now so near;
take away all human sorrow –
give us hope in place of fear.

101 UYAI MOSE

Come all you people

ZIMBABWE

Words and melody: Alexander Gondo
Music arranged John L Bell

Energetically

LEADER
WOMEN
MEN
E
A/E
U-ya-i mo-se, ti-na-ma-te Mwa-ri,
Come all you peo-ple, come and praise your Ma-ker,
U-ya-i mo-se, ti-na-ma-te Mwa-ri,
Come all you peo-ple, come and praise your Ma-ker,
Ahom
Ahom
1.
E
E/B
B7
U-ya-i mo-se, ti-na-ma-te Mwa-ri,
come all you peo-ple, come and praise your Ma-ker,
U-ya-i mo-se, ti-na-ma-te Mwa-ri,
come all you peo-ple, come and praise your Ma-ker,
Ahom
Ahom
2.
E
E/B
B7
3
except last time
D.C.
U-ya-i mo-se zvi-no. Ti-na-ma-te Mwa-ri.
come now and wor-ship the Lord. Come and praise your Ma-ker.
U-ya-i mo-se zvi-no.
come now and wor-ship the Lord.
Ahom
Ahom
Ahom

This infectious gathering song has been harmonised along traditional lines. The word *Ahom* sung by the men is simply the kind of sound without clear meaning that is common to folk music around the world. It is best taught without the singers seeing the music.

102 WA WA WA EMIMIMO

Come, O Holy Spirit, come

NIGERIA

Words and music: unknown
arranged Geoff Weaver

♩ = 88 or ♩ = 120

Capo 3(D) F (D)
Wa wa wa E-mi-mi-mo.
Come, O Ho-ly Spi-rit, come.
E-mi-o-lo-ye
Ho-ly Spi-rit, come.
Wa wa wa A-lag-ba-
Come, Al-might-y Spi-rit,
C (A)
-ra.
come.
A-lag-ba-ra me-ta
Al-might-y Spi-rit, come.
F (D) C (A) F (D)
Wa-o, wa-o, wa-o.
Come, come, come.
E-mi-mi-mo
Come, power of God.

Wa wa wa Emimimo.
Wa wa wa Alagbara.
Wao, wao, wao.

Come, O Holy Spirit, come.
Come, Almighty Spirit, come.
Come, come, come.

First 3 times: sing at slow tempo ♩ = 88: 1. top line only (with tenor response); 2. add lower alto; 3. add guitar (first beat of every bar only); 4th time onwards sing faster at ♩ = 120. Add the middle part then percussion and more rhythmic guitar.

This Yoruba invocation of the Holy Spirit is very effective when sung slowly and quietly, gradually introducing voices and instruments on each repetition as indicated. A change of tempo with drums and clapping provides an exciting conclusion, always greeted with enthusiasm by Africans.

103 WHAT WONDROUS LOVE IS THIS

UNITED STATES OF AMERICA

Words and music: American folk hymn
arranged David Peacock

Simply 𝅗𝅥 = 80
Dm C F Am7(add2) Dm
1 What wond-rous love is this, O my soul, O my
(2) God and to the Lamb, I will sing, I will
(3) when from death I'm free, I'll sing on, I'll sing
Am Fmaj7 Em7 Dm7 Am7(add2) Dm C
soul! What wond-rous love is this, O my soul! What
sing; to God and to the Lamb, I will sing. To
on, and when from death I'm free, I'll sing on. And
F B♭ Am Am7 G
wond-rous love is this that caused the Lord of bliss to
God and to the Lamb who is the great I AM, while
when from death I'm free, I'll sing and joy - ful be, and

A modal song of considerable character which should be sung simply and in unison.

Dm C F Am7(add2) Dm Am
lay a - side his crown for my soul, for my soul, to
mil - lions join the theme, I will sing, I will sing, while
through e - ter - ni - ty I'll sing on, I'll sing on, and
Fmaj7 Em7 Dm7 Am7(add2)
1.2. Dm Am7sus
3. Dm
lay a - side his crown for my soul. 2 To
mil - lions join the theme I will sing. 3 And
through e - ter - ni - ty I'll sing on.

1 What wondrous love is this,
O my soul, O my soul!
What wondrous love is this, O my soul!
What wondrous love is this
that caused the Lord of bliss
to lay aside his crown
for my soul, for my soul,
to lay aside his crown for my soul.

2 To God and to the Lamb, I will sing, I will sing;
to God and to the Lamb, I will sing.
To God and to the Lamb
who is the great I AM,
while millions join the theme,
I will sing, I will sing,
while millions join the theme I will sing.

3 And when from death I'm free,
I'll sing on, I'll sing on,
and when from death I'm free, I'll sing on.
And when from death I'm free,
I'll sing and joyful be,
and through eternity
I'll sing on, I'll sing on,
and through eternity I'll sing on.

104 WILL YOU COME AND FOLLOW ME

SCOTLAND

KELVINGROVE

Words: John L. Bell and Graham Maule
Music: Scottish melody
arranged David Peacock

Flowing ♩. = 70

Capo 3(D)
F (D) C/E (A) Dm (Bm) Am7sus (F#m)
1 Will you come and fol - low me if I but
2 Will you leave your - self be - hind if I but
3 Will you let the blind - ed see if I but
Bb (G) Gm (Em) Csus (A) C F (D)
call your name; will you go where
call your name; will you care for
call your name; will you set the
C/E (A) Dm (Bm) Am7sus (F#m) Bb2 (G) Bb/C
you don't know and ne - ver be the
cruel and kind and ne - ver be the
pris - oners free and ne - ver be the
F (D) Gm (Em) F/A (D)
same? Will you let my love be
same? Will you risk the hos - tile
same? Will you kiss the lep - er

This song may be used effectively at times of commitment.

From the *Heaven shall not wait* collection

Bbmaj7 (G)
Am7 (F#m7)
Dm7 (Bm7)
shown, will you let my name be
stare – should your life at - tract or
clean, and do such as this un -
Gm7 (Em7)
C7 (A7)
F (D)
C/E (A)
Dm (Bm)
known, will you let my life be grown in
scare? Will you let me ans - wer prayer in
- seen, and ad - mit to what I mean in
Am7sus (F#m)
Bb2 (G)
Bb/C
F (D)
you, and you in me?
you, and you in me?
you, and you in me?

4 Will you love the 'you' you hide
  if I but call your name;
will you quell the fear inside
  and never be the same?
Will you use the faith you've found
  to reshape the world around,
through my sight and touch and sound
  in you, and you in me?

5 Lord, your summons echoes true
  when you but call my name:
let me turn and follow you
  and never be the same.
In your company I'll go
  where your love and footsteps show;
thus I'll move and live and grow
  in you, and you in me.

105 WINTER HAS GONE

CHINA

Words: from Song of Solomon 2,
after Wang Wei-fan, Word & Music
Music: Jia-ou Shengben Lina
arranged Geoff Weaver

Flowing ♩. = 54
Capo 3(G)
B♭ (G) Gm (Em) B♭/D (G) F (D) B♭ (G) B♭6
1 Win - ter has gone, the night is through, flo - wers are bloom - ing,
2 Re - veal your light that I may see, your still small voice that
3 And so, my Lord, my mas - ter true, a - mong the flowers of
C7 (A7) F (D) B♭ (G) E♭ (C) B♭/D (G)
all birds sing. Why should I wait with
I may hear; and like a dove, let
pa - ra - dise I'll find you in the
E♭ (C) B♭/D (G) Cm (Am) Gm (Em) B♭/D (G) B♭ Gm (Em) B♭/D (G) F (D) Cm/E♭ (Am) Dm (Bm)
doubt and fear? A - rise, my Lord, I'll go with you!
joy and peace and love des - cend to dwell with me.
sec - ret place, and in your mer - cy go with you.

The verses of this hymn were written before the cultural revolution in China. The refrain written in 1982 sings of the dark veil of those years which brought suffering and death to so many in China, but a dramatic growth in the Church.

Chorus
F (D) Bb (G) Cm (Am) Bb (G) Eb (C) G7/D (E7) C (A)
Je - sus, my joy, my hope, my all, my love, my life
F (D) Bb (G)
e - ter - nal - ly: through death's dark night,
Eb (C) Bb/D (G) Eb (C) Bb/F (G) C7/G (A7) F7 (D7) Bb (G)
close by my side, O dear - est Lord, be close to me.

1 Winter has gone, the night is through,
flowers are blooming, all birds sing.
Why should I wait with doubt and fear?
Arise, my Lord, I'll go with you!
Jesus, my joy, my hope, my all,
my love, my life eternally:
through death's dark night, close by my side,
O dearest Lord, be close to me.

2 Reveal your light that I may see,
your still small voice that I may hear;
and like a dove, let joy and peace
and love descend to dwell with me.
Jesus, my joy . . .

3 And so, my Lord, my master true,
among the flowers of paradise
I'll find you in the secret place,
and in your mercy go with you.
Jesus, my joy . . .

106 WHAT A MIGHTY GOD WE SERVE

SOUTH AFRICA

Words: unknown
Music: Zulu working song
arranged Peter Sandwell

With strength and joy ♩ = 140

G
1 What a might - y God we serve, what a
2 He cre - a - ted you and me, he cre -
3 He has all the power to save, he has
4 Let us praise the liv - ing God, let us
5 What a might - y God we serve, what a

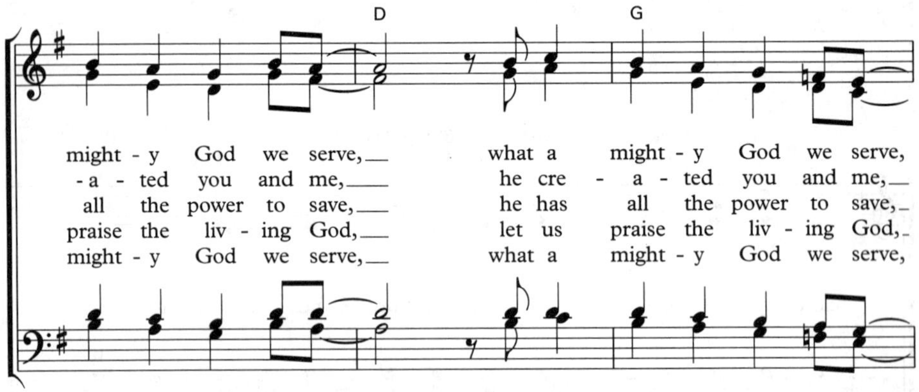
D
G
might - y God we serve, what a might - y God we serve,
- a - ted you and me, he cre - a - ted you and me,
all the power to save, he has all the power to save,
praise the liv - ing God, let us praise the liv - ing God,
might - y God we serve, what a might - y God we serve,

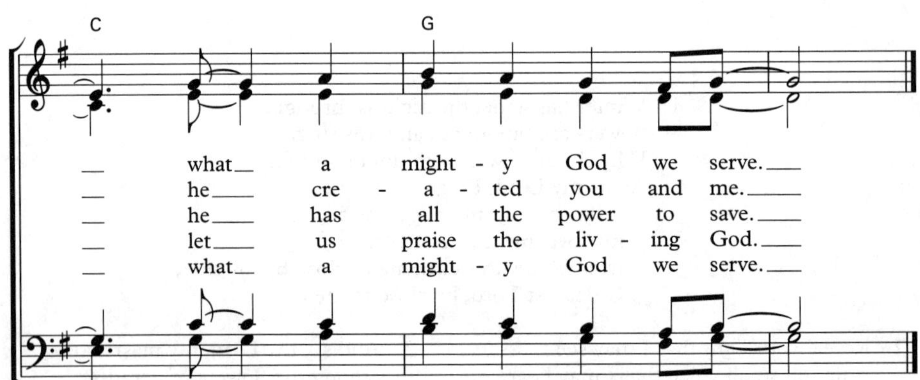
C
G
what a might - y God we serve.
he cre - a - ted you and me.
he has all the power to save.
let us praise the liv - ing God.
what a might - y God we serve.

A strong Zulu song of affirmation from South Africa.

107 YESHU SUPRIYA

Jesus, loving Lord

INDIA

Words: unknown
Music: Indian melody
arranged Geoff Weaver

1st time: vocal melody only
2nd time: vocal with accompaniment

Simply ♩ = 84

Capo 1(Bm) Cm7 (Bm7) Ab/C (G) Cm7 (Bm7) Bbmsus (Am)
Ye - shu su - pri - ya, Ye - shu a - shra - ye.
Je - sus, lov - ing Lord; Je - sus, strength and stay:
Abmaj7 (G) Gm7 (F#m) Fm9 (Em) Gm7 (F#m) Ab6 (G) Eb/Bb (D)
Ye - shu pri-ya ta - ra - ka, sa - ha - ya ho - ma - la.
in your mer-cy bless us all and keep us night and day.

Yeshu supriya,
Yeshu ashraye.
Yeshu priya taraka,
sahaya homala.

Jesus, loving Lord;
Jesus, strength and stay:
in your mercy bless us all
and keep us night and day.

A simple song of benediction from India, ideal for the end of an act of worship.

108 YOUR KINGDOM COME, O LORD

RUSSIA

Words and music: N. Zabolotski
arranged John L. Bell

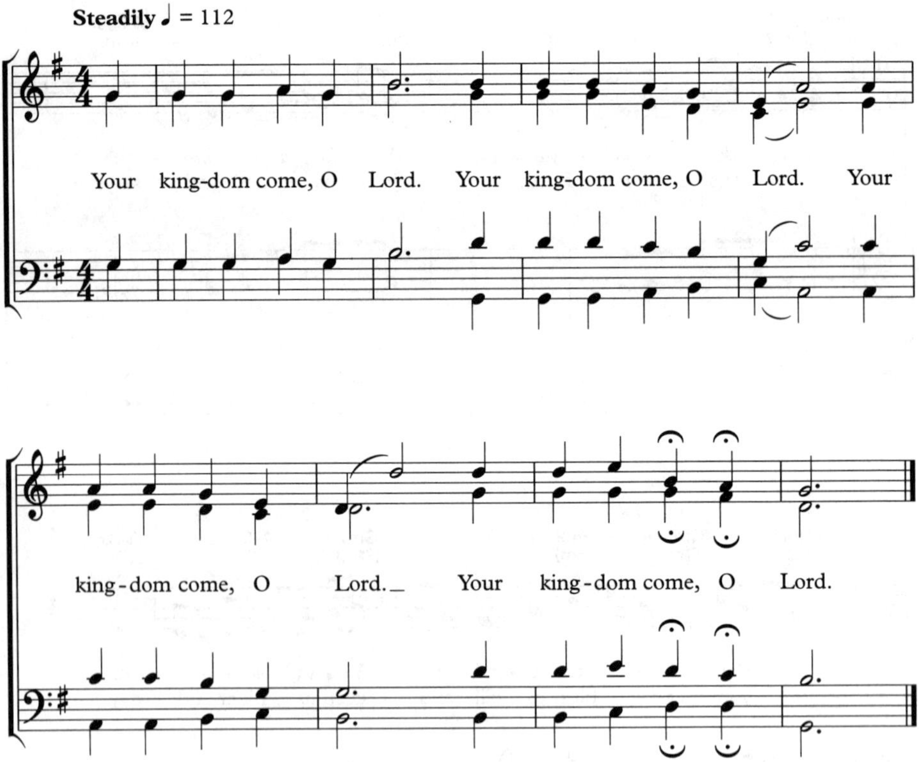
Steadily ♩ = 112
Your king-dom come, O Lord. Your king-dom come, O Lord. Your
king-dom come, O Lord._ Your king-dom come, O Lord.

Your kingdom come, O Lord.
Your kingdom come, O Lord.
Your kingdom come, O Lord.
Your kingdom come, O Lord.

Written for a W.C.C. Conference in Melbourne in 1980, the composer Nicolai Zabolotski asked that the song should start softly, almost in a questioning way, and should grow in strength and confidence until the final phrase which asserts the hope that God's Kingdom is coming.

SECTION 2:

SONGS FROM

AUSTRALIA

109 JESUS, LOVER OF MY SOUL

AUSTRALIA

Words and music: John Ezzy, Daniel Grul, Stephen McPherson

With sensitivity

G
D/F#
Baug
B7
Je - sus, lov-er of my soul,
Em
Em7
Am7
C/D
Je - sus, I will ne-ver let you go;
G
D/F#
Baug
B7
you've ta-ken me from the mi - ry clay,
Em
Em7
Am7
C/D
you've set my feet up-on the rock, and now I know:

G D/F# Em Dm7
I love you, I need you, though my world will fall, I'll
Cmaj7 C/D G
ne-ver let you go. My Sav - ior,
D/F# Em Dm7
my clos - est friend, I will wor-ship you un -
1. Cmja7 C
- til the ve - ry end.
2. Cmaj7 C C/D G
- til the ve - ry end.

110 JESUS, WHAT A BEAUTIFUL NAME

AUSTRALIA

Words and music: Tanya Riches

Flowing
D Em D/F# G
1 Je - sus, what a beau-ti-ful name — Son of
2 Je - sus, what a beau-ti-ful name — truth re -
3 Je - sus, what a beau-ti-ful name — res-cued my
D/F# G D/A Bm Em7
God, Son of Man, Lamb that was slain.
- vealed, my fu - ture sealed, healed my pain.
soul, my strong - hold, lifts me from shame.
A G D/F# G D/A
v2
v3
Joy and peace, strength and hope,
Love and free - dom, life and warmth,
For - give - ness, se - cu - ri - ty, pow - er and love,

F# F#/E Bm7 Em7 D/A
grace that blows all fear a - way: Je - sus,
grace that blows all fear a - way: Je - sus,
grace that blows all fear a - way: Je - sus,
G/A D Dsus D
what a beau - ti - ful name.
what a beau - ti - ful name.
what a beau - ti - ful name.

1 Jesus, what a beautiful name –
Son of God, Son of Man,
Lamb that was slain.
Joy and peace, strength and hope,
grace that blows all fear away:
Jesus, what a beautiful name.

2 Jesus, what a beautiful name –
truth revealed, my future sealed,
healed my pain.
Love and freedom, life and warmth,
grace that blows all fear away:
Jesus, what a beautiful name.

3 Jesus, what a beautiful name –
rescued my soul, my stronghold,
lifts me from shame.
Forgiveness, security, power and love,
grace that blows all fear away:
Jesus, what a beautiful name.

111 JUST LET ME STAY

AUSTRALIA

Words and music: Geoff Bullock

F C/E Dm Dm/C
1 Just let me say how much I love you, let me
(2) hear your fin-est whis - pers as you
(3) say how much I love you, with all my
Bb Gm7 C Dm7 C/E
speak of your mer - cy and grace, just let me
gent - ly call my name. And let me
heart I long for you. For I am
F C/E Dm Dm/C
live in the sha-dow of your beau - ty, let me
see your pow - er and your glo - ry, let me
caught in this pas - sion of know - ing this end-less
Gm7 Bb C C/Bb
see you face to face. And the
feel your Spi - rit's flame. Let me
love I've found in you. And the

Am7 Dm Dm/C
earth will shake as your word goes forth and the
find you in the des - ert till this
depth of grace, the for - give - ness found to be
Gm7 F C/E Dm7/C
hea - vens can trem - ble and fall. Just let me
sand is ho - ly ground and I am
called a child of God. Just makes me
F C/E Dm Dm/C
say how much I love you, O my
found com-plete - ly sur - ren - dered to
say how much I love you O my
B♭ C
to repeat
F
Sav - ior, my Lord and friend.
you, my Lord and friend.
Sav - ior, my Lord and friend.
Gm7 C7sus
2 Just let me
3 So let me
last time
F

112 BEAUTIFUL LORD, WONDERFUL SAVIOR

The potter's hand

AUSTRALIA

Words and music: Darlene Zschech

G
D/F#
C
1 Beau - ti - ful Lord, won-der-ful Sav - ior, I know for sure,
2 You gent-ly call me in - to your pres - ence, guid-ing me by
Cm6/Eb
Em7
Asus
A/C#
all of my days are held in your hand, craft-ed in - to your
your Ho-ly Spi - rit; teach me, dear Lord to live all of my life
Am7/D
D
Repeat 1st time only
Em
per - fect plan.
through your eyes.
I'm cap-tured by your

D/F♯ G C/G D/F♯
ho - ly call - ing: set me a - part, I know you're draw - ing me
Em Asus A Am7/D Dsus D
to your-self. Lead me, Lord, I pray.
G D/F♯ Am7
Take me, mold me, use me,
D/E Em F C/E Am7 Dsus D
fill me, I give my life to the pot - ter's hand.

G D/F# Am7 D/E Em
Call me, guide me, lead me, walk be - side me, I
F C/E Am7 G/B Dsus D
1.
D.C.
give my life to the pot - ter's hand.
2.
D.S.
3.
Am7 Dsus D Am7 G/B Dsus D G D/G
Oh
Em D/E G/F F D G
Oh Oh

113 LORD, I COME TO YOU

Power of your love

AUSTRALIA

Words and music: Geoff Bullock

Capo 2(G)
A (G)
E/G# (D/F#)
F#m (Em)
1 Lord, I come to you, let my heart be
2 Lord, un - veil my eyes, let me see you
C#m7 (Dm7)
F#m (Em)
E (D)
changed, re - newed, flow - ing from the
face to face, the know-ledge of your
D (C)
E (D)
F#m (Em)
grace that I found in you.
love as you live in me.
D/E (C/D)
E (D)
A (G)
E/G# (D/F#)
And, Lord, I've come to know
Lord, re - new my mind

the weak-ness-es I see in me
as your will un-folds in my life,
will be stripped a-way
in liv-ing ev-ery day
by the power of your love.
in the power of your love.
Chorus
Hold me close, let your love sur-round

A (G) E/G# (D/F#) F#m (Em) E (D) D (C) F#m (Em) E (D)
me, bring me near, draw me to your
A (G) Bm7 (Am7) A/C# (G/B) Em/A (Dm/G) A (G) D (C) F#m (Em)
side; and as I wait,
E (D) D (C)
I'll rise up like the ea - -
A (G) E/G# (D/F#) F#m (Em) E (D)
- gle, and I will soar with you; your Spi - rit leads me on
D (C) D/E (C/D) D/A (C/G) A (G)
in the power of your love.

114 MY JESUS, MY SAVIOR

Shout to the Lord

AUSTRALIA

Words and music: Darlene Zschech

Growing in strength
Capo 1(A)
Bb (A) F (E)
My Je - sus, my Sav - ior,
My com - fort, my shel - ter,
Gm (F#m) F (E) Eb (D)
Lord there is none like you. All of my days
tow - er of re - fuge and strength, let ev - ery breath,
Bb/D (A/C#) Eb (D) 1. Bb/F (A) Gm (F#m)
I want to praise the won - ders of your
all that I am,
Ab (G) Eb/G (D/F#) Fsus (E) F 2. Bb/F (A) Gm (F#m)
migh - ty love.
ne - ver cease to

A♭ (G) E♭/G (D) Fsus (E) F B♭ (A) Gm (F♯m)
wor - ship you. Shout to the Lord, all the earth,
I sing for joy at the work
E♭ (D) Fsus (E) F B♭ (A) Gm (F♯m)
let us sing power and ma - jes - ty, praise
of your hands. For ev - er I'll love you, for ev -
E♭ (D) Fsus (E) F Gm (F♯m)
to the King. Moun-tains bow down and the seas
- er I'll stand. Noth - ing com - pares to the prom -
1.
E♭ (D) F (E) Gm (F♯m) F/A (E)
will roar at the sound of your name.
2.
E♭ (D) F (E) B♭ (A) F/B♭ (G) E♭/B♭ (D) B♭ (A)
- ise I have in you.

115 OH, THE MERCY OF GOD

AUSTRALIA

Words and music: Geoff Bullock

G/A D G D/A A7 G/A
1 Oh, the mer - cy of God, the glo - ry of
2 Oh, the rich - ness of grace, the depths of his
3 Oh, the glo - ry of God ex-pressed in his
D D/C# Bm7 G D/F#
grace, that you chose to re - deem us, to for - give and re -
love, in him is re - demp - tion, the for - give-ness of
Son, his im - age and like - ness re - vealed to us
Asus A G/A D D/C# Bm7 D/F#
- store, and you call us your chil - dren cho - sen in
sin. You called us as right-eous, pre - des - tined in
all; the plea of the a - ges com - ple - ted in
G D/F# G D/A A7 G/A
him to be ho - ly and blame - less to the glo - ry of
him for the praise of his glo - ry, in - clu - ded in
Christ, that we be pre - sen - ted per - fec - ted in

Chorus
D G/A D A/C# Bm7
God.
Christ. To the praise of his glo - ri - ous grace,
him.
F#m/A G F#m7 Em7
to the praise of his glo - ry and power,
Asus A A/G D/F# G Bm7
to him be all glo - ry, hon - or and
Cmaj7 D/F#
praise, for ev - er and
G D/A A7 G/A D
ev - er and ev - er, A - men.

116 REFRESH MY HEART

AUSTRALIA

Words and music: Geoff Bullock

Ballad
G2 C6 G2 G/B
Re-fresh my heart, __ Lord, re-new my love,
C2 C/E D/F# G Am7 G/B F/G G
__ pour your Spi-rit in - to my soul, __
C Am7 C/D D C/D G
re-fresh my heart. __ You set me a - part,
C6 G G/B C2 C/E D/F#
__ Lord, to make me new, __

G Am7 G/B C G/D C/D D
by your Spi-rit, lift me up, Lord, re-fresh my heart.
G Am7 G/B C G
And I will wor - ship you, Lord,
C G/B Em7 G/D C
with all of my heart and I will fol -
G
- low you, Lord
1.
C Am D C/E D/F♯ G/B
re-fresh my heart,
2.
Am7 C/D E♭maj7 C/D D/F♯ D.C. G2
re-fresh my heart.

117 YOUR EYE IS ON THE SPARROW

I will run to you

AUSTRALIA

Words and music: Darlene Zschech

C D G
1 Your eye ___ is on ___ the spar - row and your hand
(2) ___ me to ___ your pur - pose, as an -
C D Em Em/D F/C C
___ it com-forts me. ___ From the ends ___ of the earth to the depths
- gels un - der - stand. ___ For your glo - ry ___ may you draw ___
D D/F# G G/B
1.
C Am7 Dsus D G/B
___ of my heart, let your mer-cy and strength be seen. ___ 2 You call
___ all ___ men, as your
2.
C Am D G
Chorus
Am/G D/F#
love ___ and grace de - mands. And I will run ___ to ___ you,

G D/F# B/D# Em G/D
— to your words_ of__ truth,_ not by__ might,
Am7 G/B C A7
— not__ by pow - er, but by the Spi - rit__ of God.
D G Am/G D/F# G
— Yes, I will run___ the__ race,__ till I see_
D/F# B/D# Em Am7
— your_ face.__ Oh, let me live___ in__ the glo -
G/B D
- ry_ of__ your grace._
to repeat
C/G D/G G
Your eye
last time
G
—

Copyright Addresses

Abingdon Press, 201 8th Ave. S., Nashville, TN 37203-3919, USA;
Telephone: +1-615-749-6000; Fax: +1-615-749-6372
Asian School of Music, Worship and the Arts, P.O. Box 10533, Quezon City 1112, Philippines
Atkins, Robert, c/o M Phillips, 24 Ty-Bryn Hill, Abertillery, Gwent, UK;
E-mail: Robert_Atkins_2@compuserve.com
Blenkinsop, Alison, 11a Grayham Road, New Maiden, Surrey KT3 5HR, England;
E-mail: blenk@hotmail.com
CanZion Producciones, S.A. de C.V. Apdo. C-62, Dgo. Mexico, C.P. 34120;
Telephone: +52-18-17-2464; Fax: +52-18-18-0779
Cartford, Gerhard, 2279 Commonwealth Ave., St. Paul, MN 55108, USA
Casa Bautista de Publicaciones, 7000 Alabama St., El Paso, TX 79904, USA;
Telephone: +1-915-566-9656; Fax: +1-915-562-6502
China Christian Council, 17 Da Jian Yin Xian, Nanjing, China;
Fax: +86-21-323-2605
Chorister's Guild, 2834 W. Kingsley Road, Garland, TX 75041, USA;
Telephone: +1-972-271-1521; Fax: +1-972-840-3113;
E-mail: choristers@choristersguild.org
Christian Conference of Asia, 96 2nd District, Pak Tin Village, Mei Tin Road, Shatin N.T., Hong Kong; Telephone: +852-2691-1068;
Fax: +852-2692-4378;
E-mail: cca@hk.super.net
The Copyright Company, 40 Music Square East, Nashville, TN 37203, USA;
Telephone: +1-615-244-5588; Fax: +1-615-244-5591
Dargie, Dave, Melusinenstrasse 13, 8000 Munchen 80, Germany
The Evangelical Lutheran Church of Finland, POB 185, 00161 Helsinki, Finland;
Telephone: +358-9-18021; Fax: +358-9-180-2350
GBG Musik, 475 Riverside Drive, New York, NY 10115, USA;
Telephone: +1-212-870-3600; Fax: +1-212-870-3748
GIA Publications, 7404 Mason Ave., Chicago, IL 60638, USA;
Telephone: +1-708-496-3800; Fax: +1-708-496-3828;
E-mail: custserv@giamusic.com
Harling, Per, Geijersgatan 18B, 752 26 Uppsala, Sweden;
E-mail: per.harling@mailbox.swipnet.se
Hope Publishing Company, 380 South Main Place, Carol Stream, IL 60188, USA; Telephone: +1-800-323-1049; Fax: +1-630-665-2552;
E-mail: hope@hopepublishing.com

Integrity's Hosanna! Music, PO Box 851622, Mobile, AL 36685-1622, USA; Telephone: +1-334-633-9000; Fax: +1-334-633-9998; E-mail: cpright@integinc.com

Laporta, Josep, C/Francisco de Miranda, 26-C 43850-CAMBRILS (TGN), Spain; Telephone: +34-929-636331; Fax: +34-977-795393; E-mail: artencel.teleline.es

Lee, Geonyong, The Korean National University of Arts, School of Music, 700 Seocho-dong, Seocho-gu, Seoul, Korea; E-mail: leegy@knua.ac.kr

Maldonodo, Jorge, Centro Hispano de Estudios Teologics, 6133 Clara Street, Bell Gardens, CA 90201, USA; Fax: +1-562-928-6983

Marashcin, Jaci, Rua Planalto 106, 09735-460 Rudge Ramos, Sao Bernardo do Campo, SP Brazil; E-mail: jmaraschin@uol.com.br

Mxandana, George, Music Director, Imilonji KaNtu Choral Society, 6942 Malie Street, PO Orlando, Soweto 1804, Johannesburg, South Africa; E-mail: georgemx@za.ibm.com

Perkio, Pia, Stenbackinkatu 5A7, SF-00250, Helsinki, Finland; E-mail: pia.perkio@kolumbus.fi

Reindorf, Dinah, PO Box 19060, Accra, Ghana

Reveil Publications, 20 rue Calliet, B.P. 4464, 69241 Lyon Cedex 04, France Telephone: +33-4-72-00-0854; Fax: +33-4-72-00-0274

Solis, Melchizedek and Mutya, 104 E. Lamar Street, Salinary, CA 93906, USA

Sosa, Pablo D., c/o Instituto Superior Evangelico, Camacua 282, Buenos Aires 1406, Argentina

Sovereign Music UK, P.O. Box 356, Leighton Buzzard, Beds. LU7 8WP, UK; Telephone: +44-1525-385578; Fax: +44-1525-372743; E-mail: SovereignM@aol.com

Turmezei, Erzsébet, 1021 Budapest, Hüvösvölgyi ut 193, Hungary

United Methodist Church Service, Mutambara, CPS Box 61, Cashel, Zimbabwe

Walton Music Corp., 170 NE 33rd Street, Fort Lauderdale, FL 33334, USA

Word Music Group, Inc., c/o Acuff-Rose Music Publishing, Inc., 65 Music Square West, Nashville, TN 37203, USA; Telephone: +1-615-321-5000; Fax: +1-615-327-0560

INDICES

COUNTRY INDEX

FIRST LINES AND TITLES INDEX